KU-054-496

First published as *The Compete Bartender's Guide* in 2003 and reprinted with updates in 2010

Second edition 2013

This edition first published in 2018

Copyright © Carlton Books Limited 2003, 2013, 2018

All rights reserved. No part of this publication may be reproduced, stored in a retrieval system, or transmitted in any form or by any means, electronic, mechanical, photocopying, recording or otherwise, without the prior permission of the copyright owner and the publishers.

A CIP catalogue record for this book is available from the British Library

ISBN 978-1-78739-170-3

Printed in China

Publisher's note:
Please use caution when using raw eggs i[n] [an]y of the recipes included in this book. Raw eggs have been known to cause salmonella poisoning and [...] women, mothers who are nursing, the eld[...] system. Readers who are pregnant or nursing children are [...] consumption.

All instructions and warnings given in [...] have made every effort to ensure that all [...]

Neither the author nor the publisher ca[...] injury, loss or damage (including any cons[...] procedures or advice offered in this book.

LONDON BOROUGH OF WANDSWORTH		
9030 00006 1925 0		
Askews & Holts	20-Sep-2018	
641.874	£11.99	
	WW18009119	

Cocktail Glasses: Key

A	B	C	D	E	F	G	H	I	J	K	L	M

A) Old-Fashioned

B) Highball

C) Collins/Tumbler

D) Shot

E) Collada

F) Brandy

G) Parfait

H) Coffee Liqueur

I) Champagne Flute

J) Martini/Cocktail

K) Champagne Saucer

L) Goblet/Wine

M) Margarita

See pages: 12–13

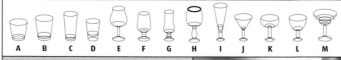

THE ESSENTIAL GUIDE
FOR MIXOLOGISTS

DAVE BROOM

CARLTON
BOOKS

Contents

Introduction

The sound is spreading around the globe. A rasping, crunching noise, like someone sprinting up a gravel path. It is a sound which had almost disappeared until recently, a black and white sound that triggered a vague memory of Hollywood movies and 1950s sitcoms, a sound made by clean-cut people enjoying each other's company, or by uniformed bartenders who knew every customer's secrets and never divulged their own. It is the sound of ice and spirits dancing together in a shaker to make a fantastical new product. It is a cocktail being born. Cocktails and cocktail bartending had almost died out in the 1970s and '80s. There were a few great hotels with top-class bartenders and a few young acolytes who keep the tradition alive in small, often private, clubs.

Cocktails were still being made, but they had slipped from mass-market consciousness along with tailfins on Cadillacs. The three Martinis sipped over a long lunch had been replaced with three mineral waters and a plate of sushi.

Thankfully, fashion is a cyclical thing and at the height of the neo-Prohibitionist movement at the start of the 1990s (it happened) a new generation began to rebel. They spurned the health fascists, demanding red meat and strong alcohol, puffing on smuggled Cuban cigars, and quaffing red wine. This is – was – a generation who want flavour, prefer to relax in quality bars, and drink quality drinks. The sound of the shaker began to get louder once more.

This book celebrates the rebirth of the cocktail. It shows that its history is one of continual evolution and re-invention and gives recipes for old classics and new drinks. Over the past 200 years a few cocktails have achieved classic status. These are described in more detail because their stories are interesting. If they can be made well, then there'll be no problem making any of the drinks in this book.

Making is the important word. This isn't just a book to flick through, but one to be used – so we look at what equipment the home bartender (on any budget) will need and how to use it. It doesn't stop there. You also have to know what ingredients go into these magical potions, not just juices, water and ice, but the whole world of alcoholic drinks.

One thing is clear when you talk to any top bartender. You can't make a great drink from cheap ingredients. The cocktail revival has, not altogether surprisingly, heralded a revival in premium spirits. Small batch bourbon, malt whisky, top-end gins, tequilas and vodkas have all appeared on the back of this.

The 21st century drinker is unlike their 1950s counterpart. Then, if you liked one type of drink you stuck with it; now, people flit from one spirit to another. The only criterion is that whatever the drink, it should be the best quality.

This is a wonderful time to be a cocktail lover. Now, get shaking!

Equipment

You can make drinks with virtually no bar equipment, but it's difficult to make great drinks with little more than the basics. You don't need to transform your living room into a proper bar, but if you want to make a good impression then it's worth investing in the essentials: a shaker, for example, the right glasses, a good range of spirits, liqueurs and bitters.

You'll want to know how to open a bottle of Champagne, how to cut a twist and flame a bit of orange peel. In time you'll realise that what turns an ordinary drink into a work of art is simply attention to detail: using orange or Peychaud bitters instead of Angostura, even just knowing how important good quality ice is. Small and inexpensive touches that make all the difference.

Cocktail Shakers

Shakers come in a mass of shapes and sizes and while it might seem like a good idea to invest in a novelty one, run three simple checks before you part with your money. Firstly, is it easy to hold? It's pointless having a baroque instrument on the bar if you drop it all the time. Secondly, is it easy to use? Does the lid get stuck, or fall off, and can you strain easily? Thirdly, is it made from stainless steel or glass? If it isn't, don't buy it.

Many bartenders use a Boston shaker. This comes in two parts: one a tall thick glass, the other similarly shaped but slightly smaller and made of stainless steel. This part fits inside the top of the glass part, allowing you to shake the ice and liquid between the two. You can also use the glass part for stirring drinks and, because it's clear, it allows you to see if your proportions are correct. Be warned, Boston shakers can be tricky to separate.

Juggling

You may, in time, decide to try and copy that hotshot barkeep you saw working the crowd in Las Vegas with his juggling tricks. My advice is DON'T. Flair bartending – as juggling bottles, glasses and shakers is known – is great fun to watch but, without wishing to be too much of a killjoy, the most important element in making a drink is making sure the drink is made correctly and tastes good. Anyway, it can make a dreadful mess of the carpet.

Glasses

There are eight glass shapes which are most widely used.

A) Shot It's fairly obvious what this glass is for. Small shots of the hard stuff intended to be drunk quickly, frozen vodka, tequila, etc. They can double up as measures if yours is lost in the fridge.

B) Old Fashioned Great for the eponymous cocktail (or variants thereof) which can be built in the glass or for old-fashioned drinks like whisky and soda.

C) Collins (Tall) The shape shows that this is a glass intended for long drinks, not just members of the **Collins** family but **Gin & Tonic** is perfect in this as are **Mojitos** and **Mint Juleps**.

D) Champagne flute The only glass for Champagne. Its shape encourages a regular, prolonged, stream of bubbles.

E) Wine glass Red wines and great whites need to breathe in the glass to release its aroma. A wide mouthed goblet not only does this but also allows you to swirl the wine to see the colour.

F) Champagne saucer A variant on the glass that is erroneously used for Champagne. Use this for any short mixed drink: **Daiquiri**, **Sours**, etc.

G) Highball Use this for making long drinks, modern, fruity cocktails, **Bloody Mary**, etc.

H) Martini (Cocktail) The classic shape for all short mixed drinks, such as **Martini** and **Manhattan**. Three rules: (1) make sure they are cold; (2) hold them by the stem while drinking (or the drink will heat up); (3) buy smaller rather than larger examples.

A   B   C   D   E

F   G   H

Blenders

Think of bartending as being like a chef. You are working with flavours, combining different ingredients to create a satisfying dish. You use knives and chopping boards. You sift, chop, strain and stir. No surprise then that many other kitchen appliances are shared by bartenders. Juicing machines are essential, while electric blenders are used for a large range of drinks: frappés for example, or frozen daiquiris. The former is served with all the ice, the latter can be served either with the ice or strained. Once you get used to making drinks in the blender another new world of flavour opens up.

It was the arrival of the electric blender that kicked off the daiquiri boom in Havana in the 1930s. It continues even today. Tony Conigliaro, one of London's top bartenders, has created a frozen gin & tonic (2 shots Tanqueray, zest of a lemon, and a splash each of tonic water, simple sugar and Cointreau) which works superbly well.

Blenders have a stainless steel cutting blade, which rotates at very high speeds meaning that you can crush ice easily (though low power domestic appliances may not be able to do this. Please check!) and also blend in fruit: strawberries, banana, melon, along with the ice and the alcohol. You could even use the blender to zap the fruit on its own. It makes a thicker drink than a juicer. There are many different brands on the market ranging in price from £29–£139 ($40–$200) and made by the majority of kitchen equipment specialists.

Fresh is best

Soda siphons, and syrup concentrates, while an integral part of American culture, are not necessary for the home bar. The key to modern cocktails is freshness, rather than concentrates and syrups, and while the addition of syrups to carbonated/"charged" water brought pleasure to not only generations of American children – and teetotallers in the nineteenth and twentieth centuries – a juicer and blender are both better for making cocktails. Bars are bars, soda siphons are soda siphons. Never the twain should meet.

Corkscrews

Like shakers these come in a bizarre range of shapes and sizes, however the simplest designs tend to be the best. Stick to the good old-fashioned corkscrew, known as the waiter's friend (far right, opposite page). It has a knife on one side for cutting the foil and a spiral and lever on the other. It works a treat, doesn't break the corks and fits neatly into your pocket.

Bar Accessories

▼ Mixing Glass This is an essential piece of kit you can't be without.

▲ Strainer To ensure that no bits of ice end up in the drink.

▼ Measuring spoons To gauge those vital small additions.

▼Measure Use a measure until you feel confident to measure by eye.

▼ Ice bucket Keep it full.

▼ **Ice scoop** To ladle in the ice when making frozen drinks.

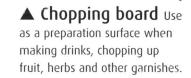

▲ **Chopping board** Use as a preparation surface when making drinks, chopping up fruit, herbs and other garnishes.

▼ **Straws** These come in different lengths and widths, depending on the type of drink being served. They are necessary for longer drinks

▲ **Sharp knife** Especially important for preparing garnishes.

▼ **Cocktail sticks** Handy for securing olives, onions, cherries and other fruit.

▲ **Swizzle sticks** Useful for stirring long drinks.

▼ **Ice tongs** Use tongs instead of your hands to pick up ice, otherwise it will melt.

Bartending at home

Once you've developed a passion for mixing drinks, the next thing you'll need is a home bar for assembling drinks. The days of improvizing in the kitchen will become a thing of the past and you'll want to perform your mixing skills in front of your friends. The area you choose to set up a home bar will depend on the layout of your house, the space available and your budget! Usually the room you use for social gatherings – the living room or den – tends to be the obvious choice for the home bar. It is entirely up to you, however, there are some practicalities to bear in mind before you set up. A large home bar is more than just a collection of bottles and glasses: it is, to all intents and purposes, a scaled- down version of a professional bar. It is up to you how much money you invest, but there are some essentials for which you will have to budget.

Case the Joint

Visit a few bars and study how they are set up. They allow bartenders to mix different drinks at the same time, without searching for ingredients. There will be a fridge under the bar top, alongside the sinks and an area for commonly used spirits.

All Mod Cons

A sink You'll need at least one, preferably two. One for washing your hands and washing up glasses, knives, chopping boards and other equipment; the other for rinsing fruit, chilling down glasses, etc.

A fridge (or, space allowing, a fridge-freezer). In this you'll keep the ice, white spirits, fruit juices, Champagne, white wine and beer.

An ice-making machine Although not essential is very useful because of the volumes of ice needed when making drinks.

A non-slip floor surface This is also advisable. Liquids tend to be spilled when making drinks and can cause accidents.

Stainless steel The best material for the bar top because it is not only easy to clean but also looks impressive. On top of the bar you should have your shakers, measures, a full basket of fruit, a blender and a juicer.

Following this principle, keep the spirits which you use the most frequently within easy reach. Store the fancy drinks, such as bourbons, tequilas, liqueurs and so on, on higher shelves and in groups. Arrange your glasses in order of use as well, storing those you require most often in the most accessible places.

Setting up your own Minibar

Not all of us have the space to dedicate a corner of a room, let alone an entire room, to mixing drinks. In any case, you can have as much fun making cocktails from a small cocktail cabinet. Look around in car-boot sales or antique shops for them; it is amazing what you can find.

The key here is to choose your spirit brands carefully and only buy the spirits and liqueurs which you know you'll use regularly. Because space is limited, restrict the number of spirits to those that work the best with the widest range of cocktails: a good quality silver, or reposado tequila will be more versatile than an expensive anejo, for example.

Store your most useful spirits in the cabinet along with your shaker, strainer, measures, and so on, and keep other less used spirits and liqueurs close by in a cupboard where you keep your glasses. Store vodka and gin in the fridge so that you also have space in your cabinet for bitters, rum, bourbon/Scotch and tequila.

In a large home bar it is possible to mix a variety of different drinks for your guests, but with a smaller set up it might be best

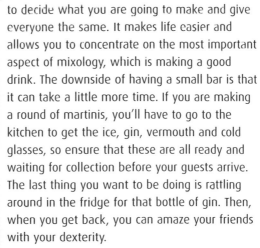

to decide what you are going to make and give everyone the same. It makes life easier and allows you to concentrate on the most important aspect of mixology, which is making a good drink. The downside of having a small bar is that it can take a little more time. If you are making a round of martinis, you'll have to go to the kitchen to get the ice, gin, vermouth and cold glasses, so ensure that these are all ready and waiting for collection before your guests arrive. The last thing you want to be doing is rattling around in the fridge for that bottle of gin. Then, when you get back, you can amaze your friends with your dexterity.

Don't drink and drive: Luxury stretch limos come with all mod cons, including a mini-bar – but don't offer the driver a cocktail!

Principles of storage

Apart from having the right bottle in the right place at the right time, good storage also involves knowing the best way to preserve a drink's freshness and character.

Spirits

Spirits are less sensitive than wines, but even they have their own peculiarities. White spirits, especially vodka and gin, should be kept in the fridge, or better still in the freezer. The cold temperature gives them a rich texture and, since cocktails are cold drinks, improves the quality of your mixed drink. Remember to stick to brands at 40% ABV and above; anything below that will freeze. Brown spirits, such as brandy, Scotch/bourbon and dark rum can be kept at room temperature.

Unlike wine, spirits do not improve in the bottle, although there are some people who claim that Chartreuse does. Usually a spirit will start to deteriorate if the bottle has been opened months or years before. This is because when air is let into the bottle the spirit starts to oxidize, the aroma flattens and loses its vibrancy. If you do have a half-full bottle of precious malt, cognac or bourbon then simply decant it into a smaller bottle. Brown spirits in clear glass bottles will lose their colour if stored for long periods in direct sunlight.

Wine

Wine storage is a slightly more complex issue. Many wines will improve in the bottle and ideally should be stored in a cellar. That said, most of us tend to drink wine soon after we buy it, which is why many wines are made to be drunk when young. Speak to your wine merchant and find out what wines will benefit from some ageing: these will include quality claret, some Californian and Australian Cabernet and Merlot, Burgundy (red and white) top German Riesling, Loire Chenin Blanc and Cabernet Franc, Rhône reds, Chianti Riserva, Barolo/Barbaresco. The same goes for Champagne, including most non-vintage brands. It really is a good idea to buy Champagne by the case and store it for a few months.

In the unlikely event...

There are many devices available which aim to preserve wine, but if you are going to finish off a bottle the next night, just replace the cork in the bottle. The Vacuvin system which sucks the air out of the bottle might save the wine from oxidizing but it also sucks the life and aroma out at the same time. Wine bars use a system which pumps nitrogen into the bottle, sealing it from the worst effects of the air, but while it is quite efficient this method is expensive.

There many myths about how to keep Champagne, such as putting a silver spoon in the neck of the bottle in order to preserve the bubbles. This is just a myth. Champagne should be sealed with a stopper and put in the fridge. The stopper won't prevent the gas from escaping – the bubbles remain in the wine for a day or so – but it does stop any odours from the fridge seeping into the wine.

What a corker

If a wine smells of wet newspaper it is corked. This is not your fault, it is not the wine merchant's fault or even the winemaker's. It is caused by a chemical (TCA) in the cork infecting the wine.

Racks and Cellars

Even if you are not intending to store wine for a long time you will need somewhere to keep the bottles. Although to begin with you may have no intention of creating a cellar, you may change your mind once you have been bitten by the wine bug. Then you'll make the big leap and be persuaded by your friendly wine merchant that you should invest in a case or two of high quality wine which needs to be aged, then comes the vintage port and, before you know it, you need a proper cellar. But before that day arrives, all you need to start with is a wine rack. You don't need to buy an expensive one, particularly since it won't be seen in a dark, cool storage place.

All you need is a simple self-assembly rack which stores the bottles on their sides. This is especially important if you are keeping the wine for a long time because you don't want the corks to dry out. It's always worthwhile asking a hotel or restaurant which is being refurbished or closed down whether they are willing to sell a wine rack to you at a good price.

If you do decide to set up a proper cellar there are certain key rules to bear in mind in terms of temperature and humidity. Wine doesn't store well in hot conditions and should be stored at temperatures below 25°C (77°F). Similarly, your cellar should not be too cold. If the temperature drops below freezing, not only could the wine freeze but also the corks may burst out of the bottles. Aim for a temperature range between 10°C (50°F) and 15°C (59°F) and avoid extreme swings in temperature. A humid cellar is vital as well. Dry conditions mean dry corks and dry corks lead to oxidized wine. If you aim for a level of around 75 per cent humidity you won't have too many problems.

All in all, you need to choose your location carefully. It's all very well already having a cellar under the house, but if it also contains your boiler then it won't be any good for storing wine. The garage may be the right size for a cellar, but it's unlikely to be sufficiently humid. A large cupboard in a spare room or study may be the right size, but check whether there are any hot water pipes running in the wall behind it because these will make the storage space too hot.

You can hire the services of a specialist firm to design and install a cellar, but first decide whether you could do it yourself by insulating a cupboard or box-room. Your trusty wine rack can be pressed into service again, although if you have large quantities of the same wine it might be easier to store them together in larger boxes or bins. Try and arrange the storage so that the wines that need the longest time to mature, such as vintage port, are positioned furthest away from the door. Those which are ready to drink should be the easiest to lay your hands on. Use your wine rack for everyday, ready-to-drink wines, and the cellar for the bottles you want to keep for years.

Bar Craft

Acocktail is a mixed drink. Classically it contains three broad parts: a base spirit which makes up the bulk of the volume and gives the drink its main flavour; a mixer, which binds it together; and the flavouring, which could be a dash of bitters, a drop of liqueur, or a squeeze of juice. Of course, it's slightly more complex than that, but the point is that a cocktail should be a balanced drink, where no single element dominates. In short, a cocktail is a drink which is greater than the sum of its parts.

Techniques and craft

Shaking

Shaking is the most effective way of mixing the ingredients, while simultaneously chilling the drink and diluting it slightly. Dilution helps to release flavours allowing them to blend together. Never fill the shaker more than halfway with ice. Shake the drink until the outside of the shaker is freezing to the touch. Cocktails should be very cold. Use ice cubes, not crushed ice, unless otherwise stated in the recipe because a drink shaken over crushed ice can quickly become too diluted.

Stirring

In general, stirring is used to marry flavours which go together easily, without making the drink cloudy, which is what happens when you shake. The principle is the same as shaking: a way to mix the ingredients together, chill a drink quickly and dilute it slightly. Half fill a shaker with ice and stir for about 20 seconds, or until the outside is chilled, then strain into cocktail glasses. Some recipes, for example the Old Fashioned, suggest the drink is stirred in the serving glasses.

Mine host: The barman is king of all he surveys and purveys to customers.

Blending

This is a good way to make long, thirst-quenching drinks. Simply whizz up the ice with the spirit ingredients and serve unstrained in the glass. Because the ice is crushed it melts more quickly and produces a fairly dilute alcoholic slush in the glass. It's a matter of personal preference. I like to taste the alcohol in the drink, but I can see the advantage of a frozen blended drink when you have a long, hot summer's afternoon ahead of you, hence the **Frozen Daiquiri.**

Muddling

Some recipes, such as **Caipirinha**, p. 74, and **Old Fashioned**, p. 158, call for "muddling" to take place. This involves pressing and mixing ingredients: mint, fruit, peel etc., in the bottom of the glass, often with bitters and over bar sugar. The rough surface of the sugar helps break up the ingredients easily. You can use the back of a spoon if you don't own a proper muddler, an implement similar to a pestle.

Layering

This process involves introducing the heaviest part of the drink first, followed by a succession of progressively lighter layers. The layers are carefully poured over the back of a spoon to sit one on top of the other. (See the **B52**, p. 51, or **Traffic Light**, p. 199).

Salting and Sugaring

The intention here is to coat the outside, not the inside, of the rim. Don't, therefore, bury the rim in a pile of salt or sugar.

Instead, moisten the outside rim with lime or lemon juice and then carefully turn the glass, side on, in a saucer of salt or sugar. Alternatively, you can sprinkle the salt or sugar onto the rim while rotating the glass, although this is a messier method.

Fruit

When using fruit for a garnish, make sure it is fresh and has been thoroughly washed. Try rolling limes and lemons before you cut them as this starts to release their juices. To cut a twist, pare small strips from a lemon ensuring there is some white pith attached. Holding the peel between thumb and forefinger give it a quick twist so that it sprays some of its oil on the surface of the drink. Run the twist round the rim of the glass and gently drop in.

Flaming

The secret of flaming brandy is to warm the glass first, either over a hot coil on the stove or by holding it under a hot tap. Pour in the brandy and ignite. To light absinthe, or high-proof vodka, hold the flame at the edge of the glass until the alcohol catches. Be aware that the flames can flare up, so ensure that your hair is not hanging over the glass.

Party Trick

One crowd-pleasing technique is to cut a section of orange peel about the size of a 10p piece. Now light a match. Hold the peel over the drink between thumb and forefinger and half snap, half flex it outwards. The spray of oils will ignite and settle on the drink giving it a wonderfully exotic flavour.

Bartenders Checklist

Alcohol

Gin (kept in fridge or freezer)
Vodka (kept in fridge or freezer)
Bison Grass vodka
Homemade flavoured vodka
White rum
Gold/aged rum
Tequila (100% blue agave silver/reposado)
Bourbon
Rye whiskey
Blended Scotch
Cognac
Noilly Prat
Red vermouth
Punt e Mes
Cointreau/curacao
Campari
Maraschino liqueur
Absinthe
Green Chartreuse
Kahlua
Champagne
Port
Fino sherry
Selection of liqueurs (amaretto, crème de cacao/menthe, etc.)
Angostura bitters
Peychaud bitters
Orange bitters
Underberg (for hangovers)

Others

Fresh limes, lemons, oranges, kumquat
Orgeat syrup
Grenadine
Freshly squeezed fruit juices
Maraschino cherries
Caster sugar
Maldon salt
Lime cordial
Tabasco
Worcestershire sauce
Horseradish
Mixers (tonic, soda, ginger ale)

A–Z of Cocktails

Here's the fun section, where all the simple, classic, exotic, and indulgent cocktails from all over the world are listed for your perusal. On the following pages you will discover tart temptations such as a Pisco Sour, sweet sensual sippers such as Bellini, and mind-how-many you-have martinis, both classic and nouveau pretenders to the title. Feature cocktails focus on classics.

Should you decide to make one or two of them, you will find the exact measurement for each ingredient and clear instructions on how to create a professional looking cocktail, shimmering and inviting in its appropriate glass.

Some cocktail names are shared by similar or completely different recipes. The variations are marked as (alt).

Cocktail Recipes

21st Century (Jim Meehan)

2 oz (60 ml/4 tbsp.) Siete Leguas Blanco tequila
¾ oz (22 ml/1½ tbsp.) lemon juice
¾ oz (22 ml/1½ tbsp.) Marie Brizard white creme de cacao
Pernod rinse
Shake all and strain into a Pernod-rinsed cocktail glass.

57 T-Bird

1 oz. (30 ml/2 tbsp.) vodka
⅔ oz. (20 ml/1⅓ tbsp.) amaretto
⅔ oz. (20 ml/1⅓ tbsp.) melon liqueur
⅔ oz. (20 ml/1⅓ tbsp.) peach schnapps
1⅔ oz. (50 ml/3⅓ tbsp.) fresh orange juice
Shake the ingredients, then strain into an ice-filled old-fashioned glass and serve.

Absolut Hero

1 oz. (30 ml/2 tbsp.) blackcurrant vodka
1 oz. (30 ml/2 tbsp.) lemon vodka
1 oz. (30 ml/2 tbsp.) melon liqueur
⅔ oz. (20 ml/1⅓ tbsp.) fresh lime juice
⅔ oz. (20 ml/1⅓ tbsp.) egg white
club soda
lime wedge to garnish
Shake the ingredients, except club soda. Strain into an ice-filled highball glass. Fill with soda and stir. Garnish with the lime wedge and serve.

Acapulco

1 oz. (30 ml/2 tbsp.) gold tequila
1 oz. (30 ml/2 tbsp.) gold rum
2 oz. (60ml/4 tbsp.) grapefruit juice
3 oz. (90ml/6 tbsp.) pineapple juice
Shake the ingredients, then strain into an ice-filled highball glass.

Adam and Eve

1 oz. (30 ml/2 tbsp.) cognac
1 oz. (30 ml/2 tbsp.) gin
1 oz. (30 ml/2 tbsp.) Forbidden Fruit liqueur
Shake the ingredients, then strain into a martini glass and serve.

Affinity

2 oz. (60 ml/4 tbsp.) Scotch whisky
1½ oz. (45 ml/3 tbsp.) sweet vermouth
1½ oz. (45 ml/3 tbsp.) dry vermouth
2 dashes Angostura bitters
twist of lemon to garnish
**Stir the whisky and vermouths in
a mixing glass, then strain into
a martini glass and serve with
the lemon twist.**

After Eight

1 oz. (30 ml/2 tbsp.) Kahlua
1 oz. (30 ml/2 tbsp.) crème de menthe
1 oz. (30 ml/2 tbsp.) crème de cacao (brown)
dash cognac
Shake the ingredients, then strain into a martini glass and serve.

Affinity

Afternoon Delight

1 oz. (30 ml/2 tbsp.) dark rum
1 oz. (30 ml/2 tbsp.) fresh orange juice
1 oz. (30 ml/2 tbsp.) coconut cream
½ oz. (15 ml/1 tbsp.) crème de fraise
½ oz. (15 ml/1 tbsp.) heavy (double) cream
6 strawberries
**Place the ingredients into a blender. Add crushed ice and blend.
Pour into a goblet and serve.**

Alabama Fizz

2 oz. (60 ml/4 tbsp.) gin
1 oz. (30 ml/2 tbsp.) fresh lemon juice
dash gomme syrup
club soda
**Shake the ingredients, except the soda, then strain into an ice-filled
highball glass. Fill with soda, stir, and serve.**

Alabama Slammer

1 oz. (30 ml/2 tbsp.) amaretto
1 oz. (30 ml/2 tbsp.) Southern Comfort
1 oz. (30 ml/2 tbsp.) sloe gin
dash fresh lemon juice
**Stir the amaretto, Southern Comfort, and
gin in a mixing glass, then strain into a shot
glass. Add the lemon juice and serve.**

Alaska

2 oz. (60 ml/4 tbsp.) gin
splash yellow Chartreuse
dash Angostura or orange bitters
lemon twist to garnish
**Shake the ingredients, then strain into a
martini glass. Add the twist and serve.**

Alaska

Alcazar

2 oz. (60 ml/4 tbsp.) Canadian Club
1 oz. (30 ml/2 tbsp.) Benedictine
dash orange bitters
Shake the ingredients, then strain into a martini glass and serve.

Alcazar (alt)

1 oz. (30 ml/2 tbsp.) vodka
1 oz. (30 ml/2 tbsp.) apricot purée
dash apricot liqueur
champagne
Shake the ingredients, except the champagne. Strain into a champagne flute. Fill with champagne, stir, and serve.

Alexander Baby

1 oz. (30 ml/2 tbsp.) Navy rum
1 oz. (30 ml/2 tbsp.) brown crème de cacao
1 oz. (30 ml/2 tbsp.) heavy (double) cream
Shake the ingredients, then strain into a martini glass and serve.

Alexander's Brother

1 oz. (30 ml/2 tbsp.) gin
1 oz. (30 ml/2 tbsp.) white crème de menthe
1 oz. (30 ml/2 tbsp.) heavy (double) cream
Shake the ingredients, then strain into a martini glass and serve.

Alexander's Other Brother

1 oz. (30 ml/2 tbsp.) gin
1 oz. (30 ml/2 tbsp.) white crème de menthe
1 oz. (30 ml/2 tbsp.) heavy (double) cream
grated nutmeg to garnish
Shake the ingredients, then strain into a martini glass. Sprinkle with nutmeg and serve.

Alexander's Sister

1 oz. (30 ml/2 tbsp.) gin
1 oz. (30 ml/2 tbsp.) green crème de menthe
1 oz. (30 ml/2 tbsp.) heavy (double) cream
Shake the ingredients, then strain into a martini glass and serve.

Alfonso

1 oz. (30 ml/2 tbsp.) Dubonnet
1 sugar cube
2 dashes Angostura bitters
champagne
Place the sugar cube in a champagne flute and soak with the Angostura bitters. Add the Dubonnet, fill with champagne, then stir.

Alfonzo

2 oz. (60 ml/4 tbsp.) Grand Marnier
1 oz. (30 ml/2 tbsp.) gin
1 oz. (30 ml/2 tbsp.) dry vermouth
½ oz. (15 ml/1 tbsp.) sweet vermouth
dash Angostura bitters
Shake the ingredients, then strain into a martini glass and serve.

Algonquin

2 oz. (60 ml/4 tbsp.) rye whiskey
1 oz. (30 ml/2 tbsp.) dry vermouth
1 oz. (30 ml/2 tbsp.) pineapple juice
dash of Peychaud bitters
Shake the ingredients, then strain into a martini glass and serve.

Allies

1 oz. (30 ml/2 tbsp.) dry vermouth
1 oz. (30 ml/2 tbsp.) gin
1 oz. (30 ml/2 tbsp.) kummel
Stir the vermouth, gin, and kummel in a mixing glass, then strain into a martini glass and serve.

Algonquin

Amaretto Comfort

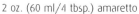

2 oz. (60 ml/4 tbsp.) amaretto
2 oz. (60 ml/4 tbsp.) Southern Comfort
1 oz. (30 ml/2 tbsp.) heavy (double) cream
Stir the amaretto and Southern Comfort in a mixing glass, then strain into a large martini glass. Float the cream on top and serve.

Amaretto Tea

6 oz. (180 ml/12 tbsp.) hot tea
2 oz. (60 ml/4 tbsp.) amaretto
whipped cream for topping
Place a spoon in a parfait glass, then pour in the hot tea. (The spoon prevents the glass from cracking.) Add the amaretto, without stirring, and top off with the whipped cream and serve.

Ambrosia

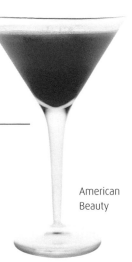

1 oz. (30 ml/2 tbsp.) calvados
1 oz. (30 ml/2 tbsp.) cognac
dash curaçao
chilled champagne

**Shake the calvados, cognac, and curaçao,
then strain into a champagne saucer.
Fill with champagne and serve.**

American Beauty

½ oz. (15 ml/1 tbsp.) brandy
¼ oz. (8 ml/½ tbsp.) dry vermouth
¼ oz. (8 ml/½ tbsp.) sweet vermouth
¾ oz. (22 ml/1½ tbsp.) fresh orange
dash grenadine
dash Crème de Menthe [optional]
½ oz. (15 ml/1 tbsp.) port

American
Beauty

**Shake the ingredients, except the port, strain
into a martini glass, float the port, and serve.**

American Coffee

1 oz. (30 ml/2 tbsp.) bourbon
6 oz. (180 ml/12 tbsp.) hot black coffee
2 tsp. raw sugar
heavy (double) cream

**Pour the bourbon and black coffee into a liqueur coffee glass,
then add the sugar. Float the cream on top and serve.**

American Fizz

1 oz. (30 ml/2 tbsp.) dark rum
1 oz. (30 ml/2 tbsp.) banana purée
1 oz. (30 ml/2 tbsp.) pineapple juice
champagne

**Shake the ingredients, except the champagne. Strain into
a champagne flute. Fill with champagne, stir, and serve.**

American Grog

2 oz. (60 ml/4 tbsp.) dark rum
½ oz. (15 ml/1 tbsp.) fresh lemon juice
1 sugar cube
Place the ingredients into a goblet. Top with hot water, stir, and serve.

Angel Face

1 oz. (30 ml/2 tbsp.) gin
1 oz. (30 ml/2 tbsp.) apricot brandy
1 oz. (30 ml/2 tbsp.) calvados
Shake the ingredients, then strain into a martini glass and serve.

Angel's Kiss

¼ oz. (8 ml/½ tbsp.) white crème de cacao
¼ oz. (8 ml/½ tbsp.) sloe gin
¼ oz. (8 ml/½ tbsp.) brandy
¼ oz. (8 ml/½ tbsp.) light (single) cream
In a shot glass, layer each of the ingredients in turn and serve.

Angelic

3 oz. (90 ml/6 tbsp.) bourbon
1 oz. (30 ml/2 tbsp.) crème de cacao
1 oz. (30 ml/2 tbsp.) Grenadine
1 oz. (30 ml/2 tbsp.) heavy (double) cream
Shake the ingredients, then strain into a double martini glass. Sprinkle on the nutmeg and serve.

Anglo Angel

1 oz. (30 ml/2 tbsp.) vodka
1 oz. (30 ml/2 tbsp.) Mandarine Napoleon
1 oz. (30 ml/2 tbsp.) mandarin juice
2 dashes Angostura bitters
Shake the ingredients, then strain into a cocktail glass and serve.

Aquamarine

1 oz. (30 ml/2 tbsp.) vodka
⅔ oz. (20 ml/1⅓ tbsp.) peach schnapps
⅓ oz. (10 ml/⅔ tbsp.) blue curaçao
⅓ oz. (10 ml/⅔ tbsp.) Cointreau
3 oz. (90 ml/6 tbsp.) apple juice
Shake the ingredients, then strain into an ice-filled old-fashioned glass and serve.

Aqueduct

3 oz. (90 ml/6 tbsp.) vodka
½ oz. (15 ml/1 tbsp.) triple sec
½ oz. (15 ml/1 tbsp.) apricot brandy
½ oz. (15 ml/1 tbsp.) fresh lime juice
Shake the ingredients, then strain into a martini glass and serve.

Aristocrat

2 oz. (60 ml/4 tbsp.) Poire William
1 oz. (30 ml/2 tbsp.) white rum
3 oz. (90 ml/6 tbsp.) pineapple juice
dash orgeat
half a pear
Blend all the ingredients, pour into a large goblet, and serve.

Aromatherapist

3 oz. (90 ml/6 tbsp.) gin
1 oz. (30 ml/2 tbsp.) sake
3 dashes Angostura bitters
Stir the ingredients in a mixing glass, then strain into a martini glass and serve.

Aster

3 oz. (90 ml/6 tbsp.) gin
dash fresh orange juice
dash fresh lemon juice

Stir the ingredients in a mixing glass, then pour into an old-fashioned glass and serve.

Astoria

2 oz. (60 ml/4 tbsp.) gin
1 oz. (30 ml/2 tbsp.) dry vermouth
dash orange bitters
Shake the ingredients, then strain into a cocktail glass and serve.

Aunt Jermina (Jemima)

1 oz. (30 ml/2 tbsp.) cognac
1 oz. (30 ml/2 tbsp.) Benedictine
1 oz. (30 ml/2 tbsp.) white crème de cacao
Pour the ingredients into a brandy glass, stir, and serve.

Aviation 2

1⅔ oz. (50 ml/1⅓ tbsp.) vodka
1 oz. (30 ml/2 tbsp.) maraschino liqueur
⅔ oz. (20 ml/1⅓ tbsp.) fresh lemon juice
maraschino cherry and a twist of lemon to garnish
Shake the ingredients, then strain into a cocktail glass. Drop the cherry in the drink, add the twist of lemon, and serve.

B-52

⅔ oz. (20 ml/1⅓ tbsp.) Tia Maria
⅔ oz. (20 ml/1⅓ tbsp.) Bailey's
⅔ oz. (20 ml/1⅓ tbsp.) Cointreau
In a shot glass, layer each of the ingredients in turn and serve.

Banana Daiquiri (see Daiquiri, p. 64–65)

1 oz. (30 ml/2 tbsp.) crème de banane
1 oz. (30 ml/2 tbsp.) white rum
1 oz. (30 ml/2 tbsp.) of fresh lime juice
½ oz. (15 ml/1 tbsp.) gomme syrup
half a banana
Blend the ingredients, then pour into a large cocktail glass and serve.

Banshee

2 oz. (60 ml/4 tbsp.) crème de banane
1 oz. (30 ml/2 tbsp.) white crème de cacao
2 oz. (60 ml/4 tbsp.) heavy (double) cream
Shake the ingredients, then strain into a goblet and serve.

Barracuda

1 oz. (30 ml/2 tbsp.) white rum
1 oz. (30 ml/2 tbsp.) Galliano
1 oz. (30 ml/2 tbsp.) pineapple juice
½ oz. (15 ml/1 tbsp.) fresh lime juice
½ oz. (15 ml/1 tbsp.) grenadine
chilled champagne
Pour all the ingredients into a highball glass, fill up with champagne, and serve.

Bastille

1 oz. (30 ml/2 tbsp.) white rum
4 blackberries
⅓ oz. (10 ml/⅔ tbsp.) crème de mure
half a slice of orange
dash gomme syrup
champagne
Muddle the berries with the gomme and crème de mure in a shaker. Add the rum. Squeeze the slice of orange over it and add ice cubes. Shake and strain into a flute. Fill with champagne. Stir and serve.

Batida

2 oz. (60 ml/4 tbsp.) cachaça
½ oz. (15 ml/1 tbsp.) gomme syrup
fresh fruit of your choice
**Blend the ingredients until chilled,
then pour into a goblet and serve.**

Bee Stinger

2 oz. (60 ml/4 tbsp.) white crème de menthe
1 oz. (30 ml/2 tbsp.) crème de cassis
**Pour the ingredients into a brandy glass.
Stir and serve.**

Bee's Kiss

2 oz. (60 ml/4 tbsp.) white rum
½ oz. (15 ml/1 tbsp.) black coffee
½ oz. (15 ml/1 tbsp.) heavy (double) cream
**Shake the ingredients, then strain into a
cocktail glass and serve.**

Bee's Kiss

Beja Flor

2 oz. (60 ml/4 tbsp.) cachaça
1 oz. (30 ml/2 tbsp.) triple sec/Cointreau
1 oz. (30 ml/2 tbsp.) crème de banane
Shake the ingredients, then strain into a cocktail glass and serve.

Belgian Coffee

1 oz. (30 ml/2 tbsp.) elixir d'anvers
6 oz. (180 ml/12 tbsp.) hot black coffee
2 tsp. raw sugar
heavy (double) cream
**Pour the elixir d'anvers and black coffee into a liqueur coffee glass,
then add the sugar. Float the cream on top and serve.**

Bloody Mary

Probably the world's best-known hangover cure
because of its unique life-giving ingredients!

This cocktail came to life in the 1920s in Harry's New York Bar in
Paris, where a bartender, Fernand Petiot, mixed vodka with tomato
juice and called it the Bloody Mary, referring to Mary Tudor.

America was introduced to the Bloody Mary after John Jacob Astor
tempted Petiot to New York to work at the St. Regis Hotel. Astor
insisted he rename it Red Snapper because he felt the word
"bloody" was too rude for customers. Because vodka was not yet
available in the U.S., Petoit used gin. However, clients liked the
name Bloody Mary so the name stuck. It's one of the great
restorative drinks. It gives enough alcohol to get you started,
but enough flavor and liquid to build you up.

No two people can agree on what should and shouldn't go into a
Bloody Mary other than vodka, tomato juice and Worcestershire
sauce. And celery stalks irritate or poke you in the eye.

Canadians substitute Clamato juice for tomato, add horseradish
sauce and celery salt, and call the result a Caesar.

Bloody Mary

2 oz. (60 ml/4 tbsp.) vodka
6 oz. (180 ml/8 tbsp.) tomato juice
2 dashes Worcestershire sauce
pinch black pepper
pinch of celery salt
½ oz. (15 ml/1 tbsp.) fresh lemon juice
Tabasco sauce (to taste)
Pour the vodka over ice in a highball
glass. Combine the other ingredients
in a jug, then add the mix to the vodka.
(A celery stick is optional!)

Bella, Bella

1 oz. (30 ml/2 tbsp.) gin
⅔ oz. (20 ml/1⅓ tbsp.) Aperol
½ oz. (15 ml/1 tbsp.) limoncello
½ oz. (15 ml/1 tbsp.) mandarin liqueur
⅔ oz. (20 ml/1⅓ tbsp.) fresh orange juice
lime spiral to garnish
Shake the ingredients, then strain into a cocktail glass. Add the lime spiral and serve.

Bellini

6 oz. (180 ml/12 tbsp.) white peach purée
  (or peach nectar)
chilled champagne
Add the peach purée to a champagne flute, fill up with champagne, and serve.

Bellini (alt)

6 oz. (180 ml/12 tbsp.) fresh white peach purée
dash fresh lemon juice
dash of peach brandy
sparkling wine
Stir the peach juice and brandy in a champagne flute. Fill up with sparkling wine and serve.

Benton Old-Fashioned (Don Lee)

2 oz (60 ml/4 tbsp.) Benton's bacon fat-infused bourbon
¼ oz (8 ml/½ tbsp.) grade B maple syrup
2 dashes Angostura bitters
orange twist to garnish
Stir all ingredients over ice, then strain over ice in a rocks glass. Garnish with orange twist.

Bermuda Rose

3 oz. (90 ml/6 tbsp.) gin
⅔ oz. (20 ml/1⅓ tbsp.) apricot brandy
⅔ oz. (20 ml/1⅓ tbsp.) grenadine
Shake the ingredients, then strain into a martini glass and serve.

Berry Sweet (Makes two)

2 oz. (60 ml/4 tbsp.) cachaça
2 small limes, diced
few raspberries
few blueberries
6 strawberries, diced and hulled
1 tbsp. brown sugar
Add the sugar and the pieces of lime to the bottom of a small bowl. Muddle the lime, releasing the juices, then add berries. Muddle some more. Place a scoop of this mixture into an old-fashioned glass. Add cachaça and crushed ice and stir. Serve with a stirrer and a straw.

Between the Sheets

1 oz. (30 ml/2 tbsp.) brandy
1 oz. (30 ml/2 tbsp.) white rum
1 oz. (30 ml/2 tbsp.) Cointreau
1 oz. (30 ml/2 tbsp.) fresh lemon juice
½ oz. (15 ml/1 tbsp.) gomme syrup
Shake the ingredients, then strain into a martini glass and serve.

Big Apple

1 oz. (30 ml/2 tbsp.) apple schnapps
1 oz. (30 ml/2 tbsp.) amaretto
1 oz. (30 ml/2 tbsp.) Drambuie
1 oz. (30 ml/2 tbsp.) fresh lemon juice
Shake the ingredients, then strain into a martini glass and serve.

Black Russian

2 oz. (60 ml/4 tbsp.) vodka
2 oz. (60 ml/4 tbsp.) Kahlua
Pour the vodka, then the Kahlua into an old fashioned glass straight up or over crushed ice, then serve.

Bloody Caesar Shooter (see Bloody Mary, pp. 50–51)

1 clam
1 oz. (30 ml/2 tbsp.) vodka
1 oz. (30 ml/2 tbsp.) tomato juice
2 drops Worcestershire sauce
2 drops Tabasco
½ tsp. horseradish purée
pinch celery salt
Put the clam in the bottom of a shot glass, then shake the rest of the ingredients in a shaker. Strain into the glass and serve.

Bloody Maria (see Bloody Mary, pp. 50–51)

2 oz. (60 ml/4 tbsp.) tequila
5 oz. (150 ml/10 tbsp.) tomato juice
juice of half a lemon
pinch celery salt
pinch black pepper
4 dashes Tabasco sauce
4 dashes Worcestershire sauce
Shake the ingredients, then strain into an ice-filled highball glass. Garnish with a celery stick and a lime wedge.

Bloody Mary (see pp. 50–51)

Blow Job

1½ oz. (45 ml/3 tbsp.) amaretto
Whipping cream
Pour the amaretto into shot glass, top with whipping cream. Drink with hands behind back in one smooth motion.

Blue Blazer

1 wineglass Scotch whisky
1 wineglass boiling water
1 tsp. sugar (to taste)
lemon twist to garnish

Warning: This cocktail requires a great degree of skill and care. Using two silver-plated mugs with handles, pour the scotch into one mug and the boiling water into the other. Ignite the whisky with a match and pour the blazing ingredients back and forth between the two mugs several times. Aim to create a long stream of liquid fire. Pour into an old-fashioned glass and add the sugar. Serve with a lemon twist.

Blue Boy

3 oz. (90 ml/6 tbsp.) dark rum
1 oz. (30 ml/2 tbsp.) sweet vermouth
dash fresh orange juice
dash orange bitters

Shake the ingredients, then strain into an old-fashioned glass and serve.

Blue Hawaiian

1 oz. (30 ml/2 tbsp.) white rum
1 oz. (30 ml/2 tbsp.) blue curaçao
3 oz. (90 ml/6 tbsp.) pineapple juice
1 oz. (30 ml/2 tbsp.) coconut cream

Blend the ingredients and pour into a large goblet and serve.

Blue Martini (see Martini, pp. 104–105)

2 oz. (60 ml/4 tbsp.) vodka
⅓ oz. (10 ml/⅔ tbsp.) blue curaçao
⅓ oz. (10 ml/⅔ tbsp.) fresh lemon juice
8 fresh blueberries

Muddle the blueberries in the bottom of a shaker. Add the remaining ingredients. Shake, then strain into a cocktail glass and serve.

Blue Monday

1 oz. (30 ml/2 tbsp.) gin
1 oz. (30 ml/2 tbsp.) Cointreau
dash blue curaçao
club soda
**Pour the gin and the Cointreau into a
highball with ice, then fill with club soda.
Stir. Add a dash of blue curaçao. Stir and
serve with a stirrer.**

Bombay Bellini

6 oz. (180 ml/12 tbsp.) fresh white peach purée
2 oz. (60 ml/4 tbsp.) mango purée
dash fresh lemon juice
dash of peach brandy
sparkling wine
**Stir peach juice and brandy in a
champagne flute. Add the mango
purée, fill up with the sparkling wine,
stir, and serve.**

Bombay
Bellini

Bonza Monza

1 oz. (30 ml/2 tbsp.) vodka
⅔ oz. (20 ml/1⅓ tbsp.) crème de cassis
2 oz. (60 ml/4 tbsp.) grapefruit juice
**Pour the ingredients into an old-fashioned glass full of crushed ice.
Stir and serve.**

Boston Bullet

2 oz. (60 ml/4 tbsp.) chilled dry gin
spray of Noilly Prat from an atomizer
olive stuffed with an almond to garnish
**Spray a chilled martini glass with Noilly Prat then add the gin.
Add the olive and serve.**

Boston Bullet (alt)

2 oz. (60 ml/4 tbsp.) chilled vodka
spray of Noilly Prat from an atomizer
olive stuffed with an almond to garnish
**Spray a chilled martini glass with Noilly Prat then add the vodka.
Add the olive and serve.**

Brandy Alexander

1 oz. (30 ml/2 tbsp.) cognac
1 oz. (30 ml/2 tbsp.) brown crème de cacao
1 oz. (30 ml/2 tbsp.) heavy (double) cream
**Shake the ingredients, then strain into a
martini glass and serve.**

Brandy Alexander (alt)

1 oz. (30 ml/2 tbsp.) cognac
1 oz. (30 ml/2 tbsp.) brown crème de cacao
1 oz. (30 ml/2 tbsp.) heavy
   (double) cream
whipped cream
grated nutmeg to garnish
**Shake the first three ingredients, then strain
into a cocktail glass. Add the whipped cream
and sprinkle nutmeg to garnish.**

Brandy
Alexander

Brandy Cocktail

2 oz. (60 ml/4 tbsp.) cognac
1 oz. (30 ml/2 tbsp.) sweet vermouth
2 dashes Angostura bitters
**Stir the cognac, vermouth, and bitters in a mixing glass, then strain
into a martini glass and serve.**

Brandy Eggnog

2 oz. (60 ml/4 tbsp.) cognac
1 oz. (30 ml/2 tbsp.) dark rum
1 oz. (30 ml/2 tbsp.) gomme syrup
1 egg
3 oz. (90 ml/6 tbsp.) milk
grated nutmeg to garnish
Stir the cognac, rum, gomme syrup, and egg in a mixing glass, then strain into a goblet. Stir in the milk and sprinkle the grated nutmeg over the top.

Brandy Smash

2 oz. (60 ml/4 tbsp.) cognac
1 tsp. granulated sugar
6–8 fresh mint leaves
Dissolve the sugar with a dash of the cognac in the bottom of an old-fashioned glass. Add the mint and muddle. Fill with ice and stir in the remaining cognac until the glass has become frosted. Serve with a short straw.

Brave Bull

1⅓ oz. (40 ml/2⅔ tbsp.) tequila
⅔ oz. (20 ml/1⅓ tbsp.) coffee liqueur
Pour ingredients into an old-fashioned glass with ice. Stir and serve.

Breakfast Bar

2 oz. (60 ml/4 tbsp.) vodka
handful cherry tomatoes
1 fresh basil leaf
pinch ground coriander
pinch celery salt
chopped chives
pinch ground pepper
Blend the ingredients, then strain into an ice-filled highball and serve.

Breezy Nik (Chris Edwardes)

1 oz. (30 ml/2 tbsp.) vodka
½ oz. (15 ml/1 tbsp.) gin
1 oz. (30 ml/2 tbsp.) pear schnapps
juice of half a lemon
½ oz. (15 ml/1 tbsp.) blackcurrant purée
4 oz. (120 ml/8 tbsp.) cranberry juice
**Shake the ingredients, then strain
into a highball glass and serve.**

Brighton Punch

1 oz. (30 ml/2 tbsp.) bourbon
2 oz. (60 ml/4 tbsp.) orange juice
3 oz. (90 ml/6 tbsp.) brandy
¼ oz. (8 ml/⅓ tbsp.) Benedictine
¾ oz. (24 ml/1½ tbsp.) lemon juice
1 tsp. gomme syrup
**Shake the ingredients,
then strain into an ice-filled
highball glass and serve.**

Brighton
Punch

Brighton Rock

2 oz. (60 ml/4 tbsp.) crème de fraise
3 oz. (90 ml/6 tbsp.) cranberry juice
1 oz. (30 ml/2 tbsp.) heavy (double) cream
Shake the ingredients, then pour into a highball glass and serve.

Broadway Martini
(see Martini, pp. 104–105)

2 oz. (60 ml/4 tbsp.) gin
½ oz. (15 ml/1 tbsp.) white
crème de menthe
**Shake the ingredients, then strain into a Martini
glass.**

Bronx

1 oz. (30 ml/2 tbsp.) gin
½ oz. (15 ml/1 tbsp.) sweet vermouth
½ oz. (15 ml/1 tbsp.) dry vermouth
juice of quarter of an orange
slice of orange to garnish
**Shake the ingredients, then strain into
a martini glass. Add the orange slice
and serve.**

Bronx

Bronx View

1⅔ oz. (50 ml/3⅓ tbsp.) gin
1 oz. (30 ml/2 tbsp.) dry vermouth
⅓ oz. (10 ml/⅔ tbsp.) Rose's Lime Cordial
**Shake the ingredients, then strain into
a cocktail glass and serve.**

Brooklyn

1 oz. (30 ml/2 tbsp.) rye whiskey
¾ oz. (22 ml/1½ tbsp.) vermouth rosso
dash of maraschino liqueur
**Mix the ingredients in a mixing glass.
Strain into a martini glass and serve.**

Brooklyn

Buck's Fizz

2 oz. (60 ml/4 tbsp.) fresh orange juice
chilled champagne
**Pour the orange juice into a champagne flute, fill up with champagne,
and serve.**

Bullshot (see Bloody Mary, pp. 50–51)

1⅔ oz. (50 ml/3⅓ tbsp.) vodka
5 oz. (150 ml/10 tbsp.) beef bouillon
dash fresh lemon juice
2 to 3 dashes Worcestershire sauce
celery salt
Tabasco sauce
ground black pepper
**Shake the bouillon, lemon juice, Tabasco, and Worcestershire sauces
with the vodka. Strain into an ice-filled highball. Add black pepper
to taste. Serve with a stirrer.**

Buster

3 oz. (90 ml/6 tbsp.) dark Puerto
Rican rum
1 oz. (30 ml/2 tbsp.) Pernod
pineapple chunks to garnish
**Shake the ingredients, then pour into
an old-fashioned glass. Garnish with
the pineapple and serve.**

Butterfly

2 oz. (60 ml/4 tbsp.) gin
1 oz. (30 ml/2 tbsp.) dry vermouth
1 oz. (30 ml/2 tbsp.) blue curaçao
1 oz. (30 ml/2 tbsp.) Poire William
**Shake the ingredients, then strain into
a large martini glass and serve.**

Butterfly

Butterscotch Cocktail (Chris Stock)

¾ oz (22 ml/1½ tbsp.) Butter-washed Monkey Shoulder whisky
½ oz (15 ml/1 tbsp.) Aperol
⅛ oz (5 ml/1 tsp.) PX sherry
⅛ oz (5 ml/1 tsp.) ginger jam
2 dashes Peychaud's Bitters
orange twist to garnish
Shake all and strain into a cocktail glass.

Cactus Pear Margarita (see Margarita, pp. 92–93)

2 oz. (60ml/4 tbsp.) tequila
⅔ oz. (20 ml/1⅓ tbsp.) Cointreau
⅓ oz. (10 ml/⅔ tbsp.) fresh lime juice
1 cactus pear, peeled and diced
lime wedge to garnish
Muddle the pear in the bottom of a shaker. Add a scoop of ice and other ingredients. Shake, then strain into a cocktail glass with a salted rim. Add the lime wedge and serve.

Cadillac Lady

1 oz. (30 ml/2 tbsp.) gin
1 oz. (30 ml/2 tbsp.) Grand Marnier
1 oz. (30 ml/2 tbsp.) fresh lemon juice
1 egg white
Shake the ingredients, then strain into a martini glass and serve.

Cadiz

1 oz. (30 ml/2 tbsp.) dry sherry
1 oz. (30 ml/2 tbsp.) crème de mure
½ oz. (15 ml/1 tbsp.) triple sec
½ oz. (15 ml/1 tbsp.) heavy (double) cream
Shake the ingredients, then strain into an ice-filled old-fashioned glass and serve.

Caesar (see Bloody Mary, pp. 50–51)

2 oz. (60 ml/4 tbsp.) Absolut Pepper vodka
5 oz. (150 ml/10 tbsp.) Clamato juice
2 dashes Worcestershire sauce
horseradish sauce
pinch white pepper
pinch celery salt
splash of fino sherry
splash of lemon juice
Tabasco sauce to taste
**Pour the vodka into an ice-filled highball glass. In a jug, combine
the other ingredients, then add to the vodka and ice. Stir and serve.**

Café de Paris

2 oz. (60 ml/4 tbsp.) gin
½ oz. (15 ml/1 tbsp.) light (single) cream
½ oz. (15 ml/1 tbsp.) anisette
1 egg white
Shake the ingredients, then strain into a martini glass and serve.

Café Normandie

1 oz. (30 ml/2 tbsp.) calvados
6 oz. (180 ml/12 tbsp.) hot black coffee
2 tsp. raw sugar
heavy (double) cream
**Pour the calvados and black coffee into a liqueur coffee glass,
then add the sugar. Float the cream on top and serve.**

Daiquiri

The drink, from the fashionable isle of Cuba, with a glamorous tastiness that makes it sing.

Rum's magical combination of delicate sweetness with an alcoholic kick makes it a great base for cocktails, and in the 1920s, Havana was cocktail nirvana. There, bartender Constante Ribailagua perfected a cocktail that had originally been invented in the mines in the Daiquiri mountain range in the south of the country. It was there, according to legend, that two engineers called Pagliuchi and Cox mixed together rum, lime juice, sugar, and ice.

Constante created the frozen Daiquiri, although his original is far from the mushy slush on offer today. He used crushed ice, but strained the drink rather than let the ice cause dilution in a glass.

His creation was to inspire author Ernest Hemingway—the most famous regular at el Floridita—although by the time Papa penned Islands in the Stream, ice was floating on the top.

Blenders increased the possibilities, and fresh fruit was combined with the basic recipe. Try it with bananas, mango, strawberry, raspberry, and mint.

Daiquiri

2 oz. (60 ml/4 tbsp.) white rum
juice of 1 lime
1 tsp. sugar
lemon twist to garnish
**Shake the ingredients, then
strain into a cocktail glass, add
the garnish, and serve.**

Café Royale

1 oz. (30 ml/2 tbsp.) cognac
6 oz. (180 ml/12 tbsp.) hot black coffee
2 tsp. raw sugar
heavy (double) cream
**Pour the cognac and black
coffee into a liqueur coffee
glass, then add the sugar.
Float the cream on top
and serve.**

Caipirinha

1 lime
2 oz. (60 ml/4 tbsp.) cachaça
3 sugar lumps
**Cut the lime into eighths, then
muddle with the sugar in an
old-fashioned glass. Fill the glass with
crushed ice and pour in the cachaça. Stir
and serve with two straws.**

Caipirinha

Caipirovska (An interpretation of the
Caipirinha with a tart lime flavour)

2 oz. (60 ml/4 tbsp.) vodka
1 lime, diced
dash fresh lime juice
2 tsp. superfine (caster) sugar
**Muddle the diced lime and the sugar in an old-fashioned glass. Add
the vodka and the lime juice. Fill the glass with ice, stir, and serve
with two straws.**

Cajun Martini (see Martini, pp. 104–105)

2 oz. (60 ml/4 tbsp.) chilled dry gin
spray of Noilly Prat from an atomizer
jalapeno chili to garnish
**Spray a chilled martini glass with Noilly Prat. Add the gin.
Garnish with the chili and serve.**

Cajun Martini (alt) (see Martini, pp. 104–105)

2 oz. (60 ml/4 tbsp.) chilled vodka
spray of Noilly Prat from an atomizer
jalapeno chili to garnish
**Spray a chilled martini glass with Noilly Prat. Add the vodka.
Garnish with the chili and serve.**

Cajun Martini (Paul Prudhomme) (see Martini, pp. 104–105)

1 fresh chili
1 bottle dry gin
1 oz. (30 ml/2 tbsp.) dry vermouth
**Slice the chili lengthwise, keeping it in one piece, and insert into a
bottle of gin. Top the bottle up with vermouth. Reseal and refrigerate
for up to sixteen hours. Strain into a clean bottle. Refrigerate until
well chilled. Serve in cocktail glasses.**

Calypso Coffee

1 oz. (30 ml/2 tbsp.) Tia Maria
6 oz. (180 ml/12 tbsp.) hot black coffee
2 tsp. raw sugar
heavy (double) cream
**Pour the Tia Maria and black coffee into a liqueur coffee glass,
then add the sugar. Float the cream on top and serve.**

Campbeltown Cocktail (Mike Aikman)

1½ oz (45 ml/3 tbsp.) Springbank 10YO whisky
½ oz (15 ml/1 tbsp.) Cherry Heering
¼ oz (8 ml/½ tbsp.) Green Chartreuse
lemon twist to garnish
**Stir all ingredients over ice, then strain into a Martini glass.
Garnish with lemon twist (discard).**

Canadian Coffee

1 oz. (30 ml/2 tbsp.) Canadian Club
6 oz. (180 ml/12 tbsp.) hot black coffee
2 tsp. raw sugar
heavy (double) cream
**Pour the Canadian Club and black coffee into a liqueur coffee glass,
then add the sugar. Float the cream on top and serve.**

Cape Codder

1½ oz. (45 ml/3 tbsp.) vodka
3 oz. (90 ml/6 tbsp.) cranberry juice
1 wedge of lime
**Pour vodka and cranberry juice into a highball glass over ice.
Stir well, add the lime, and serve.**

Cargo

2 oz. (60 ml/4 tbsp.) vodka
1 oz. (30 ml/2 tbsp.) white crème de menthe
2 fresh mint leaves
**Rub the rim of an old-fashioned glass with one of the mint leaves.
Pour the crème de menthe and vodka into the glass and stir. Garnish
with the other mint leaf and serve.**

Caribbean Coffee

1 oz. (30 ml/2 tbsp.) white rum
6 oz. (180 ml/12 tbsp.) hot black coffee
2 tsp. raw sugar
heavy (double) cream
Pour the rum and black coffee into a liqueur coffee glass, then add the sugar. Float the cream on top and serve.

Caribbean Royale

½ oz. (15 ml/1 tbsp.) white rum
½ oz. (15 ml/1 tbsp.) crème de banane
chilled champagne
Pour the rum and the crème de banane into a champagne flute. Fill up with champagne, stir, and serve.

Caruso

1 oz. (30 ml/2 tbsp.) gin
¾ oz. (22 ml/1½ tbsp.) dry vermouth
¼ oz. (8 ml/½ tbsp.) green crème
   de menthe
Stir the ingredients in a mixing glass, then strain into a martini glass and serve.

Caruso

Casablanca

2 oz. (60 ml/4 tbsp.) white rum
1 oz. (30 ml/2 tbsp.) Cointreau
1 oz. (30 ml/2 tbsp.) fresh lime juice
dash orange bitters
dash Maraschino liqueur [optional]
Shake the ingredients, then strain into a martini glass and serve.

Casanova

1 oz. (30 ml/2 tbsp.) apple juice
1 oz. (30 ml/2 tbsp.) raspberry purée
champagne
raspberries to garnish
**Pour the raspberry purée into a flute.
Add the apple juice and stir. Fill with champagne. Stir. Drop two small raspberries into
the drink.**

Castro

1½ oz. (45 ml/3 tbsp.) gold rum
¾ oz. (22 ml/1½ tbsp.) calvados
1½ oz. (45 ml/3 tbsp.) orange juice
¾ oz. (22 ml/1½ tbsp.) lime juice
¾ oz. (22 ml/1½ tbsp.) Rose's
   Lime Cordial
1 tsp. gomme syrup
wedge of lime

Castro

**Shake the ingredients, then strain into an ice-filled highball glass.
Garnish with the lime and serve.**

Celery Sour (Jason Scott)

2 oz (60 ml/4 tbsp.) Hendrick's gin
1 oz (30 ml/2 tbsp.) lemon juice
½ oz (15 ml/1 tbsp.) pineapple juice
½ oz (15 ml/1 tbsp.) sugar syrup
barspoon Bitter Truth celery bitters
1 egg white
celery shaving to garnish
**Dry-shake all ingredients without
ice. Shake with ice, then double-
strain into a cocktail glass. Garnish
with celery shaving.**

Centenario

1½ oz. (45 ml/3 tbsp.) gold rum
1 oz. (30 ml/2 tbsp.) overproof white rum
¼ oz. (8 ml/½ tbsp.) Kahlua
¼ oz. (8 ml/½ tbsp.) Cointreau
dash grenadine
juice of one lime
sprig of mint to garnish

Stir the ingredients and pour over ice into a highball glass. Garnish with the mint and serve.

Ceres Joker (Ryan Chetiyawardana)

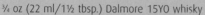

¾ oz (22 ml/1½ tbsp.) Dalmore 15YO whisky
¾ oz (22 ml/1½ tbsp.) sloe gin
¾ oz (22 ml/1½ tbsp.) lemon juice
½ oz (15 ml/1 tbsp.) sugar syrup
1 egg white
8 drops ginger bitters
Lemon scented helium balloon and magician's string to garnish

Dry-shake all ingredients without ice. Shake with ice, then double-strain into a cocktail glass. Garnish with balloon tethered to glass. Light fuse before drinking.

Chambord Kamikaze

3 oz. (90 ml/6 tbsp.) vodka
½ oz. (15 ml/1 tbsp.) Cointreau
½ oz. (15 ml/1 tbsp.) lemon juice
½ oz. (15 ml/1 tbsp.) simple syrup
½ oz. (15 ml/1 tbsp.) Chambord
half a lime, diced
slice of lime to garnish

Place the ingredients, including the diced lime, in a shaker. Muddle violently. Strain, then pour into a cocktail glass. Garnish with a slice of lime and serve.

Champagne Cocktail

chilled champagne
1 white sugar cube
dash Angostura bitters
twist of lemon peel
wedge of orange

Place the sugar cube into a flute and add a dash of Angostura. Pour in the champagne. Add the lemon twist, garnish with the orange, and serve.

Champagne Cocktail (Classic)

1 oz. (30 ml/2 tbsp.) cognac
1 white sugar cube
4 dashes Angostura bitters
chilled champagne
maraschino cherry

In a champagne flute soak the sugar cube in the Angostura bitters. Pour on the cognac and fill up with champagne. Drop in the cherry and serve.

Champagne
Cocktail

Champagne Cooler

1 oz. (30 ml/2 tbsp.) Grand Marnier
½ oz. (15 ml/1 tbsp.) cognac
2 dashes Angostura bitters
chilled champagne
slice of orange to garnish

Pour the Grand Marnier, cognac, and bitters into a champagne flute. Stir. Fill up with champagne, garnish with the orange slice, and serve.

Champagne Cup

1 bottle chilled champagne
3 oz. (90 ml/6 tbsp.) Grand Marnier
3 oz. (90 ml/6 tbsp.) cognac
dash maraschino liqueur
sliced fruits in season and several fresh mint leaves to garnish
**Mix the ingredients in a large jug containing 10–15 ice cubes.
Stir in the fruit and mint, then serve in champagne flutes.**

Champagne Julep

6 fresh mint leaves
1 tsp. powdered sugar
dash cognac
chilled champagne
**Muddle the mint and sugar with the cognac in a deep
champagne saucer. Fill up with champagne and serve.**

Champers

1 oz. (30 ml/2 tbsp.) brandy
⅔ oz. (20 ml/1⅓ tbsp.) fresh orange juice
⅔ oz. (20 ml/1⅓ tbsp.) fresh lemon juice
champagne
**Shake the first three ingredients, then
strain into a champagne flute. Stir. Fill
with champagne and serve.**

Chapala

1½ oz. (45 ml/3 tbsp.) tequila
dash triple sec
¾ oz. (22 ml/1½ tbsp.) lemon juice
2 oz. (60 ml/4 tbsp.) orange juice
dash grenadine
**Stir over ice in a highball glass
and serve.**

Chapel Hill

3 oz. (90 ml/6 tbsp.) bourbon
1 oz. (30 ml/2 tbsp.) triple sec
dash fresh lemon juice
twist of orange to garnish
Shake the ingredients, then strain into a martini glass and serve with the orange twist.

Charlie Chaplin

1 oz. (30 ml/2 tbsp.) apricot brandy
1 oz. (30 ml/2 tbsp.) sloe gin
1 oz. (30 ml/2 tbsp.) fresh lemon juice
Shake the ingredients, then strain into a martini glass and serve.

Charlotte Rose (Iain Griffiths)

1¼ oz (38 ml/2½ tbsp.) pisco
½ oz (15 ml/1 tbsp.) lime
¼ oz (8 ml/½ tbsp.) Yellow Chartreuse
⅙ oz (5 ml/1/3 tbsp.) creme de violette
⅙ oz (5 ml/1/3 tbsp.) grenadine
3 dashes Peychaud's Bitters
Shake and strain into a cocktail glass.

Chartreuse Dragon

2 oz. (60 ml/4 tbsp.) vodka
2 oz. (60 ml/4 tbsp.) lychee juice
⅔ oz. (20 ml/1⅓ tbsp.) green chartreuse
⅓ oz. (10 ml/⅔ tbsp.) blue curaçao
dash fresh lime juice
lemon & lime soda
Shake the ingredients, except the lemon & lime soda. Strain into an ice-filled highball glass. Fill with lemon & lime soda, stir, and serve.

Cherry Picker

1 oz. (30 ml/2 tbsp.) gold tequila
1 oz. (30 ml/2 tbsp.) cherry brandy
juice of half a lime
1 oz. (30 ml/2 tbsp.) apple juice
twist of lime to garnish
Shake the ingredients, then strain into a cocktail glass. Add the twist of lime and serve.

Chi Chi

2 oz. (60 ml/4 tbsp.) vodka
1 oz. (30 ml/2 tbsp.) coconut cream
3 oz. (90 ml/6 tbsp.) pineapple juice
Blend all the ingredients, then pour into a large goblet and serve.

Chicago

2 oz. (60 ml/4 tbsp.) brandy
½ oz. (15 ml/1 tbsp.) triple sec
dash Angostura bitters
Shake the ingredients, then pour into a sugar-rimmed old-fashioned glass and serve.

Chime (Ryan Chetiyawardana)

2 oz (60 ml/4 tbsp.) Hibiki 12 Japanese whisky
1 oz (30 ml/2 tbsp.) fresh lemon juice
½ oz (15 ml/1 tbsp.) grenadine
2 dashes Peychaud's Bitters
¼ oz (8 ml/½ tbsp.) orange bell pepper
1 egg white
slice pepper to garnish
Muddle pepper, then add all other ingredients. Dry-shake without ice, then shake hard with ice. Double-strain into a cocktail glass and garnish with a slice of bell pepper.

Cool Gold

1 oz. (30 ml/2 tbsp.) melon liqueur
1 oz. (30 ml/2 tbsp.) gold tequila
1 oz. (30 ml/2 tbsp.) cranberry juice
Shake the ingredients, then strain into a martini glass and serve.

Cool Martini (see Martini, pp. 104–105)

2 oz. (60 ml/4 tbsp.) vodka
⅔ oz. (20 ml/1⅓ tbsp.) apple juice
½ oz. (15 ml/1 tbsp.) Cointreau
1 oz. (15 ml/1 tbsp.) fresh lemon juice
Shake the ingredients, then strain into a martini glass and serve.

Coolcumber (Chris Edwardes)

2 oz. (60 ml/4 tbsp.) cucumber vodka
chunk of cucumber
1 oz. (30 ml/2 tbsp.) grapefruit juice
juice of a lime
½ oz. (15 ml/1 tbsp.) gomme syrup
Blend the ingredients in an ice-filled container until frozen, then pour into a large goblet and serve.

Copenhagen

2 oz. (60 ml/4 tbsp.) vodka
½ oz. (15 ml/1 tbsp.) akvavit
a few slivered blanched almonds
Shake the ingredients, then strain into a cocktail glass, garnish with the almonds, and serve.

Cordless Screwdriver

1 oz. (30 ml/2 tbsp.) chilled vodka
1 orange wedge sugar
Coat the orange wedge in the sugar and pour the vodka into a shot glass. Drink the vodka, then eat the orange.

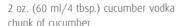

Corpse Reviver

¾ oz. (22 ml/1½ tbsp.) brandy
¾ oz. (22 ml/1½ tbsp.) calvados
¾ oz. (22 ml/1½ tbsp.) sweet vermouth
**Shake the ingredients, then strain
into a cocktail glass and serve.**

Cosmopolitan

2 oz. (60 ml/4 tbsp.) vodka
1 oz. (30 ml/2 tbsp.) Cointreau
½ oz. (15 ml/1 tbsp.) lime juice
splash cranberry juice
lime twist to garnish
**Stir the ingredients in a mixing glass, then
strain into a chilled cocktail glass with a
sugared rim. Garnish with the twist and serve.**

Cosmopolitan

Cosmopolitan (alt)

1 oz. (30 ml/2 tbsp.) vodka
½ oz. (15 ml/1 tbsp.) triple sec
½ oz. (15 ml/1 tbsp.) cranberry juice
juice of 1 lime
flamed orange peel to garnish
**Shake the ingredients, then strain into a cocktail glass and serve with
the flaming garnish.**

Cuba Libre

1⅔ oz. (50 ml/3⅓ tbsp.) white rum
juice of 1 fresh lime
cola
lime wedge to garnish
**Pour the juice, then the rum into an ice-filled highball glass.
Fill with cola. Add a wedge of lime and serve with a stirrer.**

Manhattan

When it comes to classic aperitifs with a powerful taste, we'll take Manhattan, thanks all the same.

While its name is a clear indication of where this classic whiskey cocktail was created, no-one knows who invented the Manhattan. The idea that it was Winston Churchill's mother has been debunked. What is apparent is that it predates the Dry Martini. At its heart beats the essential ingredients of nineteenth-century cocktails: sweet vermouth and bitters.

There is almost as much debate over Manhattans as there is over dry Martinis, but while the cocktail has undoubtedly become drier over the years, it should not be a dry drink. The magnificence of the Manhattan lies in the way the bitters and sweetness join in an unlikely alliance to round off the whiskey's more abrasive edges. The original recipe was probably made with rye whiskey—a style which is re-establishing itself—but bourbon is commonly used. The light style of Canadian whisky has to be carefully balanced.

But which brand? That's a matter of personal preference. Speaking personally, I'd choose Wild Turkey when I need a weighty belt of liquor after a tough day, or Maker's Mark for sophisticated sipping.

Manhattan

2 oz. rye whiskey
1 oz. sweet vermouth
3 dashes Angostura
drop of maraschino juice
maraschino cherry
Stir the ingredients in a mixing glass, then strain into cocktail glass. Drop the cherry in the glass and serve.

Cuban

2 oz. (60 ml/4 tbsp.) white rum
dash apricot brandy
juice of half a lime
dash gomme syrup
**Stir the rum, brandy, lime juice, and gomme syrup in a mixing glass.
Strain into a martini glass and serve.**

Cuban Cutie

2 oz. (60 ml/4 tbsp.) white rum
⅔ oz. (20 ml/1⅓ tbsp.) passion fruit juice
3 oz. (90 ml/6 tbsp.) grenadine
3 oz. (90 ml/6 tbsp.) fresh orange juice
lime wedge to garnish
**Shake the ingredients, then strain into an ice-filled highball glass.
Garnish with the lime wedge and serve.**

Cuban Island

¾ oz. (22 ml/1½ tbsp.) white rum
¾ oz. (22 ml/1½ tbsp.) vodka
¾ oz. (22 ml/1½ tbsp.) Cointreau
¾ oz. (22 ml/1½ tbsp.) lemon juice
Shake the ingredients, then strain into a cocktail glass and serve.

Czarina

2 oz. (60 ml/4 tbsp.) vodka
1 oz. (30 ml/2 tbsp.) apricot brandy
½ oz. (15 ml/1 tbsp.) dry vermouth
dash Angostura bitters
**Stir the ingredients in a mixing glass, then strain into a martini glass
and serve.**

Daiquiri (see p. 64–65)

Dandy

2 oz. (60 ml/4 tbsp.) Dubonnet
1 oz. (30 ml/2 tbsp.) bourbon
1 oz. (30 ml/2 tbsp.) Cointreau
dash Angostura bitters
Shake the ingredients, then strain into a martini glass and serve.

Dawn

1 oz. (30 ml/2 tbsp.) gin
⅔ oz. (20 ml/1⅓ tbsp.) Campari
1⅔ oz. (50 ml/3⅓ tbsp.) fresh orange juice
Shake the ingredients, then strain into an old-fashioned glass over crushed ice and serve.

Death Flip (Chris Hysted)

1 oz (30 ml/2 tbsp.) blanco tequila
½ oz (15 ml/1 tbsp.) Jägermeister
½ oz (15 ml/1 tbsp.) Yellow Chartreuse
½ oz (15 ml/1 tbsp.) sugar syrup
1 whole egg
nutmeg to garnish
Dry-shake all ingredients without ice. Shake with ice, then double-strain into a cocktail glass. Garnish with grated nutmeg.

Deauville

1 oz. (30 ml/2 tbsp.) brandy
¾ oz. (22 ml/1½ tbsp.) calvados
½ oz. (15 ml/1 tbsp.) triple sec
¾ oz. (22 ml/1½ tbsp.) fresh lemon juice
Shake the ingredients and strain into a cocktail glass, and serve.

Dynamite

½ oz. (15 ml/1 tbsp.) cognac
½ oz. (15 ml/1 tbsp.) Grand Marnier
1 oz. (30 ml/2 tbsp.) fresh orange juice
chilled champagne
Pour the cognac, Grand Marnier, and orange juice into a champagne flute. Stir. Fill up with champagne and serve.

East India

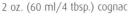

2 oz. (60 ml/4 tbsp.) cognac
½ oz. (15 ml/1 tbsp.) dark rum
dash triple sec
dash pineapple juice
dash Angostura bitters
Shake the ingredients, then strain into a martini glass and serve.

Eclipse

1 oz. (30 ml/2 tbsp.) sloe gin
1 oz. (30 ml/2 tbsp.) gin
dash grenadine
1 olive
dash fresh lemon juice
Put the olive in a martini glass, cover with the grenadine. Shake the gin and lemon, strain into the glass, not disturbing the grenadine, and serve.

Eggnog

2 oz. (60 ml/4 tbsp.) cognac
1 egg
½ oz. (15 ml/1 tbsp.) gomme syrup
dash dark rum
5 oz. (150 ml/10 tbsp.) light (single) cream
grated nutmeg to garnish
Shake the ingredients, then strain into a highball glass. Sprinkle with grated nutmeg and serve.

El Diablo

2 oz. (60 ml/4 tbsp.) silver tequila
1 oz. (30 ml/2 tbsp.) crème de cassis
juice of one lime
ginger ale
lime wedge to garnish
Pour the ingredients into a highball with crushed ice. Fill with ginger ale. Add the lime wedge and serve with a straw.

El Presidente

2 oz. (60 ml/4 tbsp.) white rum
1 oz. (30 ml/2 tbsp.) fresh lime juice
dash grenadine
dash pineapple juice
Shake the ingredients, then strain into a cocktail glass and serve.

El Diablo

Eldorado

2 oz. (60 ml/4 tbsp.) gold tequila
1 oz. (30 ml/2 tbsp.) fresh lemon juice
1 tsp. honey
Shake the ingredients, then strain into a martini glass and serve.

Elixir

1 oz. (30 ml/2 tbsp.) Grand Marnier
1 oz. (30 ml/2 tbsp.) sweet vermouth
dash Punt e Mes
2 dashes Angostura bitters
Pour the ingredients into an old-fashioned glass, stir, and serve.

Epernay

1 oz. (30 ml/2 tbsp.) crème de framboise
dash Midori melon liqueur
chilled champagne
Pour the crème de framboise and melon liqueur into a champagne flute. Fill up with champagne and serve.

The Escalador (Iain Griffiths)

1½ oz (45 ml/3 tbsp.) Calle 23 Reposado tequila
¾ oz (22 ml/1½ tbsp.) Dolin dry
½ oz (15 ml/1 tbsp.) Aperol
¼ oz (8 ml/½ tbsp.) Yellow Chartreuse
lemon twist to garnish
Stir all ingredients over ice, then strain into a Martini glass. Garnish with lemon twist.

Evans

2 oz. (60 ml/4 tbsp.) bourbon
1 oz. (30 ml/2 tbsp.) Cointreau
1 oz. (30 ml/2 tbsp.) apricot brandy
Stir the bourbon, Cointreau, and brandy in a mixing glass, then strain into an ice-filled old-fashioned glass and serve.

Evita

1 oz. (30 ml/2 tbsp.) vodka
1 oz. (30 ml/2 tbsp.) melon liqueur
2 oz. (60 ml/4 tbsp.) fresh orange juice
1 oz. (30 ml/2 tbsp.) fresh lime juice
dash gomme syrup
Shake the ingredients, then strain into an old-fashioned glass filled with ice and serve.

Filby

2 oz. (60 ml/4 tbsp.) gin
1 oz. (30 ml/2 tbsp.) Campari
1 oz. (30 ml/2 tbsp.) dry vermouth
1 oz. (30 ml/2 tbsp.) amaretto
Stir the ingredients in a mixing glass, then strain into a martini glass and serve.

Final Ward (Phil Ward)

¾ oz (22 ml/1½ tbsp.) rye whiskey
¾ oz (22 ml/1½ tbsp.) Green Chartreuse
¾ oz (22 ml/1½ tbsp.) Maraschino liqueur
¾ oz (22 ml/1½ tbsp.) lemon juice
lemon twist to garnish
Shake all ingredients, strain into a cocktail glass and garnish with lemon twist.

Fizzing Americano

1 oz. (30 ml/2 tbsp.) Campari
½ oz. (15 ml/1 tbsp.) sweet vermouth
champagne or Prosecco (Italian sparkling wine)
orange wheel to garnish
Shake the ingredients, then pour over ice in a highball glass. Fill up with champagne, add the orange, and serve.

Flirt

1 oz. (30 ml/2 tbsp.) vodka
1 oz. (15 ml/1 tbsp.) black sambuca
2 oz. (60 ml/4 tbsp.) cranberry juice
Shake the ingredients, then strain into a cocktail glass and serve.

Fizzing
Americano

85

Floridita

1½ oz. (45 ml/3 tbsp.) white rum
½ oz. (15 ml/1 tbsp.) sweet vermouth
dash of white crème de cacao
dash of grenadine
juice of half a lime
Shake the ingredients, then strain into a cocktail glass and serve.

Floridita

Flying Dutchman

3 oz. (90 ml/6 tbsp.) Dutch gin
dash triple sec
Shake the ingredients, then strain into an ice-filled old-fashioned glass and serve.

Fortunella

1 oz. (30 ml/2 tbsp.) Ketel One vodka
¾ oz. (22 ml/1½ tbsp.) Bombay Sapphire gin
¾ oz. (22 ml/1½ tbsp.) Caravella
splash Cointreau
splash Campari
1 tsp. candied kumquat nectar
twist of lemon to garnish
twist of kumquat to garnish
Coat the shaker with the Cointreau and Campari, and then discard the excess. Shake the rest of the ingredients, then strain into a cocktail glass and serve with the garnish.

Fragile Baby

1 oz. (30 ml/2 tbsp.) frangelico
2 oz. (60 ml/4 tbsp.) Bailey's
2 tsp. raw sugar
1 oz. (30 ml/2 tbsp.) heavy (double) cream
Pour the frangelico, Bailey's, and sugar into a liqueur coffee glass. Float the cream on top, then serve.

Fraises Royale

2 strawberries
1 oz. (30 ml/2 tbsp.) crème de fraise
chilled champagne
Blend the strawberries with the liqueur, then pour into a champagne flute. Fill with champagne and serve.

French 125

1 oz. (30 ml/2 tbsp.) cognac
½ oz. (15 ml/1 tbsp.) fresh lime juice
chilled champagne
twist of lime to garnish
Mix the cognac and lime juice in a champagne flute. Fill with champagne, garnish, and serve.

French 75

¾ oz. (22 ml/1½ tbsp.) gin
¼ oz. (8 ml/½ tbsp.) fresh lemon juice
dash gomme syrup
dash grenadine
champagne
Shake the first four ingredients, then strain into a champagne flute, fill with champagne, and serve.

French 75 (alt)

1½ oz. (45 ml/3 tbsp.) gin
1½ oz. (45 ml/3 tbsp.) fresh lemon juice
chilled champagne
twist of lemon to garnish
Mix the gin and lemon juice in a champagne flute. Fill with champagne, garnish, and serve.

French 75

Frozen Margarita (see Margarita, pp. 92–93)

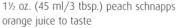

2 oz. (60 ml/4 tbsp.) tequila
1oz. (30 ml/ 2 tbsp) Cointreau
juice of half a lime
juice of half a lemon
**Blend the ingredients with crushed ice until frozen, then pour into
a margarita glass. You can add any fruit to turn this drink into a
frozen margarita.**

Fuzzy Navel

1½ oz. (45 ml/3 tbsp.) peach schnapps
orange juice to taste
**Pour peach schnapps into an ice-filled Collins glass. Fill with orange
juice and stir to combine.**

Gaelic Coffee

1 oz. (30 ml/2 tbsp.) Scotch whisky
6 oz. (180 ml/12 tbsp.) hot black coffee
2 tsp. raw sugar
heavy (double) cream
**Pour the whisky and black coffee into a liqueur coffee glass, then add
the sugar. Float the cream on top and serve.**

Gastown (Geoff Robinson)

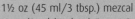

1½ oz (45 ml /3 tbsp.) mezcal
¼ oz (8 ml /½ tbsp.) Fernet Branca
¼ oz (8 ml /½ tbsp.) Cynar
⅛ oz (5 ml /1 tsp.) maple syrup
2 dashes Angostura bitters
1 dash Decanter Bitters
Stir all and strain into a cocktail glass.

The Gatsby (Andrea Montague)

1½ oz (45 ml/3 tbsp.) Plymouth Gin
½ oz (15 ml/1 tbsp.) Kamm and Sons ginseng spirit
½ oz (15 ml/1 tbsp.) nettle cordial
3 dashes Regan's Orange Bitters
Stir and strain into a cocktail glass. Garnish with lemon twist.

German Coffee

1 oz. (30 ml/2 tbsp.) kirsch
6 oz. (180 ml/12 tbsp.) hot black coffee
2 tsp. raw sugar
heavy (double) cream
Pour the kirsch and black coffee into a liqueur coffee glass, then add the sugar. Float the cream on top and serve.

Giada

1 oz. (30 ml/2 tbsp.) vodka
½ oz. (15 ml/1 tbsp.) Campari
½ oz. (15 ml/1 tbsp.) Galliano
dash pineapple juice
Shake the ingredients, then strain into a cocktail glass and serve.

Gimlet

2 oz. (60 ml/4 tbsp.) gin or vodka
1 oz. (30 ml/2 tbsp.) lime cordial
wedge of lime to garnish
Pour the spirit and lime cordial over ice cubes in an cocktail glass and serve.

Gimlet

89

...der

1 oz. (30 ml/2 tbsp.) gin
1 oz. (30 ml/2 tbsp.) brown crème de cacao
1 oz. (30 ml/2 tbsp.) heavy (double) cream
**Shake the ingredients, then strain
into a martini glass and serve.**

Gin Basil Smash (Jorg Meyer)

3 oz (90 ml/6 tbsp.) Hendrick's gin
1 oz (30 ml/2 tbsp.) lemon juice
⅔ oz (20 ml/1⅓ tbsp.) sugar syrup
1 bunch basil
basil leaf to garnish
**Add all ingredients to a shaker,
then muddle basil into liquid.
Shake hard, double-strain over ice
in a rocks glass, and garnish with
basil leaf.**

Ginger Jest

1 oz. (30 ml/2 tbsp.) bourbon
1 oz. (30 ml/2 tbsp.) pineapple juice
2 to 3 slices fresh ginger
champagne
**Muddle the ginger in a shaker. Add the bourbon, pineapple juice,
and ice cubes. Shake and strain into a champagne flute. Fill with
champagne, stir, and serve.**

Gloom Raiser

2 oz. (60 ml/4 tbsp.) gin
1 oz. (30 ml/2 tbsp.) vermouth
2 dashes grenadine
2 dashes absinthe or Pernod
Shake the ingredients, then strain into a cocktail glass and serve.

Goddess

1 oz. (30 ml/2 tbsp.) Pernod
1 oz. (30 ml/2 tbsp.) amaretto
**Shake the Pernod and amaretto, then strain into a martini glass
and serve.**

Godfather

2 oz. (60 ml/4 tbsp.) Scotch whisky
1 oz. (30 ml/2 tbsp.) amaretto
Pour the scotch and amaretto into an old-fashioned glass and serve.

Godmother

2 oz. (60 ml/4 tbsp.) vodka
1 oz. (30 ml/2 tbsp.) amaretto
Pour the vodka and amaretto into an old-fashioned glass and serve.

Golden Apple (Chris Edwardes)

1 oz. (30 ml/2 tbsp.) Mount Gay rum
½ oz. (15 ml/1 tbsp.) apple schnapps
1 oz. (30 ml/2 tbsp.) apple purée
juice of 1 lime
½ oz. (15 ml/1 tbsp.) gomme syrup
Shake the ingredients, then strain into a martini glass and serve.

Golden Cadillac

1 oz. (30 ml/2 tbsp.) crème de cacao
1 oz. (30 ml/2 tbsp.) Galliano
1 oz. (30 ml/2 tbsp.) heavy (double) cream
Shake the ingredients, then strain into a martini glass and serve.

Margarita

This was the first tequila cocktail and there is no other with its ability to stimulate the appetite.

The Margarita has been rather overlooked in the brave new world of the postmodern cocktail. This is partly because it was abused by unfeeling and uncaring bartenders during the 1970s and 1980s, who turned it from a lip-smacking aperitif that cleared your head and made your eyes gleam, into a glorified slush puppy.

The cocktail had a refined history before the madmen with their blenders got hold of it. Legend recounts that it was invented by Margaret Sames, an American socialite of the 1940s, who used to serve it at parties in Acapulco. A similar drink was already popular in Mexico before Margaret's husband graciously attached her name to it.

The first Margarita was a mix of tequila, Cointreau, and lime juice. The best Margaritas still follow this basic recipe. Just like Daiquiris, though, as soon as the blenders began to be wielded with reckless abandon, so fruit began to be whizzed into the mix. Strawberry is a common variant, although the best I ever tasted was a blueberry one. Experiment, but don't use too much ice in the blender!

Margarita

2 oz. (60 ml/4 tbsp.) gold tequila
1 oz. (30 ml/2 tbsp.) Cointreau or
  triple sec
juice of half a lime
juice of half a lemon
**Shake the ingredients, then strain
into a salt-rimmed margarita glass
and serve.**

Golden Margarita (see Margarita, p. 92–93)

2 oz. (60 ml/4 tbsp.) gold tequila
1 oz. (30 ml/2 tbsp.) Grand Marnier
juice of 1 lime
lime wedge to garnish
Shake the ingredients, then strain into a margarita glass with a salted rim. Add the lime wedge and serve.

Good Fellow

1 oz. (30 ml/2 tbsp.) cognac
1 oz. (30 ml/2 tbsp.) Benedictine
2 dashes Angostura bitters
½ oz. (15 ml/1 tbsp.) gomme syrup
Shake the ingredients, then strain into a martini glass and serve.

Goose Bumps

1 oz. (30 ml/2 tbsp.) vodka
1 oz. (30 ml/2 tbsp.) red cherry purée
dash cherry liqueur
champagne
Pour the vodka, cherry purée, and cherry liqueur into a champagne flute. Stir, then fill with champagne. Stir and serve.

Grand Mimosa

2 oz. (60 ml/4 tbsp.) Grand Marnier
1 oz. (30 ml/2 tbsp.) fresh orange juice
chilled champagne
Pour the Grand Marnier and orange juice into a champagne flute, stir, then fill with champagne and serve.

Grapefruit Daiquiri (see Daiquiri, p. 64–65)

2 oz. (60 ml/4 tbsp.) white rum
1 oz. (30 ml/2 tbsp.) fresh grapefruit juice
dash gomme syrup
**Shake the ingredients, then strain
into a cocktail glass and serve.**

Green Beast (Charles Vexenat)

1 oz (30 ml/2 tbsp.) Pernod Absinthe
1 oz (30 ml/2 tbsp.) lime juice
4 oz (120 ml/8 tbsp.) water
1 oz (30 ml/2 tbsp.) sugar syrup
Cucumber to garnish
**Build in a highball glass over ice.
Garnish with slices of cucumber.**

Green Dinosaur

⅔ oz. (20 ml/1⅓ tbsp.) vodka
⅔ oz. (20 ml/1⅓ tbsp.) gold tequila
⅔ oz. (20 ml/1⅓ tbsp.) light rum
⅔ oz. (20 ml/1⅓ tbsp.) gin
⅔ oz. (20 ml/1⅓ tbsp.) triple sec
1 oz. (30 ml/2 tbsp.) fresh lime juice
dash gomme syrup
dash melon liqueur
**Shake the ingredients, except the melon liqueur, and strain into an
ice-filled highball. Float the melon liqueur over the top and serve.**

Green Point (Mickey McIlroy)

2 oz (60 ml/4 tbsp.) Rittenhouse bonded rye
1 oz (30 ml/2 tbsp.) Punt e Mes
⅛ oz (5 ml/1 tsp.) Yellow Chartreuse
1 dash Angostura bitters
Stir all and strain into a cocktail glass.

Gumdrop

2 oz. (60 ml/4 tbsp.) Scotch whisky
1 oz. (30 ml/2 tbsp.) Galliano
Pour the scotch and Galliano into an old-fashioned glass, stir, and serve.

H. G. Wells

2 oz. (60 ml/4 tbsp.) bourbon
1 oz. (30 ml/2 tbsp.) dry vermouth
½ oz. (15 ml/1 tbsp.) Pernod
2 dashes Angostura bitters
Stir the ingredients in a mixing glass, then strain into an ice-filled old-fashioned glass and serve.

Hair of the Dog

2 oz. (60 ml/4 tbsp.) Scotch whisky
1 oz. (30 ml/2 tbsp.) honey
1 oz. (30 ml/2 tbsp.) heavy (double) cream
Shake the ingredients, then strain into a martini glass and serve.

Hair Raiser

2 oz. (60 ml/4 tbsp.) 100 proof vodka
1½ oz. (45 ml/3 tbsp.) rye whiskey
½ oz. (15 ml/1 tbsp.) fresh lemon juice
Shake the ingredients, then strain into a martini glass and serve.

Half and Half

2 oz. (60 ml/4 tbsp.) dry vermouth
2 oz. (60 ml/4 tbsp.) sweet vermouth
twist of lemon to garnish
Pour the vermouths into an old-fashioned glass, stir, then garnish with the lemon twist and serve.

Happy Birthday

1 oz. (30 ml/2 tbsp.) Cointreau
1 oz. (30 ml/2 tbsp.) blue curaçao
½ oz. (15 ml/1 tbsp.) Galliano
½ oz. (15 ml/1 tbsp.) white rum
Stir the ingredients in a mixing glass, then strain into a martini glass and serve.

Happy Youth

2 oz. (60 ml/4 tbsp.) cherry brandy
1 oz. (30 ml/2 tbsp.) fresh orange juice
1 sugar cube
chilled champagne
cherry to garnish
Pour the cherry brandy and orange juice over the sugar cube in a flute. Fill with champagne. Garnish with the cherry and serve.

Harmony

2 oz. (60 ml/4 tbsp.) cognac
½ oz. (15 ml/1 tbsp.) crème de fraises
2 dashes orange bitters
dash maraschino liqueur
Stir the ingredients in an old-fashioned glass and serve.

Harper Cranberry

2 oz. (60 ml/4 tbsp.) I. W. Harper bourbon
3 oz. (90 ml/6 tbsp.) cranberry juice
Stir the ingredients in a mixing glass, then strain into an ice-filled highball glass.

Harper
Cranberry

Harry's Cocktail

2 oz. (60 ml/4 tbsp.) gin
1 oz. (30 ml/2 tbsp.) sweet vermouth
dash pastis
1 sprig of mint
Shake the ingredients, then strain into a martini glass and serve.

Harvey Wallbanger

2 oz. (60 ml/4 tbsp.) vodka
5 oz. (150 ml/10 tbsp.) fresh orange juice
1 oz. (30 ml/2 tbsp.) Galliano
slice of orange
Pour the vodka and orange juice into an ice-filled highball and stir. Float the Galliano on top. Garnish with the orange and serve with a stirrer.

Harvey
Wallbanger

Hemingway

1 oz. (30 ml/2 tbsp.) Pernod
chilled champagne
Pour the Pernod into a champagne flute, then fill with champagne and serve.

Holy Trinity (Ryan Chetiyawardana)

2 oz (60 ml/4 tbsp.) No 3 gin
¼ oz (8 ml/½ tbsp.) Petit Chablis
knifepoint dried wormwood
radish to garnish
Stir all ingredients over ice, then strain into a Martini glass. Garnish with radish.

Honeymoon Paradise

1 oz. (30 ml/2 tbsp.) blue curaçao
1 oz. (30 ml/2 tbsp.) Cointreau
1 oz. (30 ml/2 tbsp.) fresh lemon juice
chilled champagne
Pour the blue curaçao and Cointreau into a high-ball glass. Fill with champagne and serve.

Horse's Neck

2 oz. (60 ml/4 tbsp.) bourbon
2 dashes Angostura bitters
ginger ale
twist of lemon
Coat a highball glass with bitters. Add ice and the bourbon. Stir, then fill with ginger ale and the lemon twist. Stir briefly and serve.

Horse's
Neck

Hot Brandy Alexander

1 oz. (30 ml/2 tbsp.) brandy
1 oz. (30 ml/2 tbsp.) brown crème
  de cacao
4 oz. (120 ml/8 tbsp.) steamed milk
whipped cream
chocolate shavings to garnish
Pour the brandy, crème de cacao, and milk into a heatproof glass. Top with the whipped cream and chocolate shavings, then serve.

Hot Brandy Flip

2 oz. (60 ml/4 tbsp.) cognac
½ oz. (15 ml/1 tbsp.) gomme syrup
1 egg yolk
4 oz. (120 ml/8 tbsp.) hot milk
grated nutmeg to decorate
Mix the cognac, gomme syrup, and egg yolk in a highball glass. Stir in the hot milk and sprinkle with the nutmeg.

Hot Eggnog

1 oz. (30 ml/2 tbsp.) dark rum
1 oz. (30 ml/2 tbsp.) cognac
1 oz. (30 ml/2 tbsp.) gomme syrup
1 egg
6 oz. (180 ml/12 tbsp.) hot milk
grated nutmeg to garnish
**Shake the rum, cognac, gomme syrup, and egg, then strain into a
highball glass. Stir in the hot milk, sprinkle with the nutmeg, and serve.**

Hot Pants

2 oz. (60 ml/4 tbsp.) tequila
1 oz. (30 ml/2 tbsp.) peppermint schnapps
½ oz. (15 ml/1 tbsp.) grapefruit juice
**Shake the ingredients, then pour into a salt-rimmed old-fashioned glass
and serve.**

Hot Toddy

1 lemon wheel
6 cloves
1 oz. (30 ml/2 tbsp.) Scotch whisky
1 oz. (30 ml/2 tbsp.) fresh lemon juice
1 tsp. brown sugar
dash orgeat syrup
1 cinnamon stick
boiling water
**Stud the lemon wheel with the cloves and put in a heatproof goblet.
Add the rest of the ingredients, then fill up with boiling water. Stir with
the cinnamon stick and serve.**

Hot Buttered Rum

1 tsp. brown sugar
boiling water
1 tsp. butter
2 oz. (60 ml/4 tbsp.) dark rum
grated nutmeg to garnish

Put the brown sugar in a heatproof glass and fill to two-thirds full with boiling water. Stir in the butter and rum, then sprinkle with the nutmeg and serve.

Hurricane

1 oz. (30 ml/2 tbsp.) white rum
1 oz. (30 ml/2 tbsp.) dark rum
⅔ oz. (20 ml/1⅓ tbsp.) triple sec
juice of 1 lime
⅔ oz. (20 ml/1⅓ tbsp.) gomme syrup
⅓ oz (10 ml/⅔ tbsp.) grenadine
3 oz. (90 ml/6 tbsp.) fresh orange juice
3 oz. (90 ml/6 tbsp.) pineapple juice

Shake the ingredients, then strain into an ice-filled highball glass and serve.

Hurricane (alt)

1 oz. (30 ml/2 tbsp.) dark rum
1 oz. (30 ml/2 tbsp.) white rum
½ oz. (15 ml/1 tbsp.) grenadine
2 dashes fresh lime juice

Shake the ingredients, then strain into a martini glass and serve.

Italian Coffee

1 oz. (30 ml/2 tbsp.) Strega
6 oz. (180 ml/12 tbsp.) hot black coffee
2 tsp. raw sugar
heavy (double) cream
**Pour the Strega and black coffee into a liqueur coffee glass, then add
the sugar. Float the cream on top and serve.**

Itza Paramount

1 oz. (30 ml/2 tbsp.) gin
1 oz. (30 ml/2 tbsp.) Drambuie
1 oz. (30 ml/2 tbsp.) Cointreau
**Stir the gin, Drambuie, and Cointreau in a mixing glass, then strain into
a martini glass and serve.**

Jack Rabbit

2 oz. (60 ml/4 tbsp.) applejack or calvados
dash fresh lemon juice
dash fresh orange juice
dash gomme syrup
Shake the ingredients, then strain into a martini glass and serve.

Jack Zeller

1 oz. (30 ml/2 tbsp.) Old Tom gin
1 oz. (30 ml/2 tbsp.) Dubonnet
**Stir the gin and Dubonnet in a mixing glass, then strain into a martini
glass and serve.**

Iceberg

2 oz. (60 ml/4 tbsp.) vodka
dash Pernod
**Stir the vodka and Pernod in a mixing glass, then pour into an ice-filled
old-fashioned glass and serve.**

Jacuzzi

1 oz. (30 ml/2 tbsp.) gin
⅔ oz. (20 ml/1⅓ tbsp.) peach schnapps
1 oz. (30 ml/2 tbsp.) fresh orange juice
champagne
**Shake the ingredients, except the champagne, and strain into
a champagne flute. Fill with champagne. Stir and serve.**

Jade Lady

1 oz. (30 ml/2 tbsp.) gin
1 oz. (30 ml/2 tbsp.) blue curaçao
1 oz. (30 ml/2 tbsp.) advocaat
1⅓ oz. (40 ml/2⅔ tbsp.) fresh orange juice
**Shake the ingredients, then strain into a cocktail
glass and serve.**

James Bond

1 oz. (30 ml/2 tbsp.) vodka
1 sugar cube
3 dashes Angostura bitters
chilled champagne
**Place the sugar cube in a champagne
flute and soak in the bitters, then
pour on the vodka. Fill with champagne
and serve.**

Japanese Garden (Hidetsugu Ueno)

1½ oz (45 ml/3 tbsp.) Hakushu 12YO whisky
¾ oz (22 ml/1½ tbsp.) Midori
½ oz (15 ml/1 tbsp.) Hermes Green Tea liqueur
Stir and strain over ice in a rocks glass.

James
Bond

Martini (Dry)

James Bond is entirely responsible for the myth that a Martini should be shaken, not stirred.

Gin is the original cocktail spirit and in the late nineteenth century gave the world its most famous cocktail—the dry Martini. It may have started life as a dry version of the Martinez, which itself was a variation of the Gin Cocktail. Both were sweet drinks. It could even, as suggested by Anistatia Miller and Jared Brown, have taken its name from Martini Dry Vermouth.

The Martini began as an equal mix between gin and vermouth; now the ratio is anywhere from 4:1 to 25:1. The aim is to get a drink that has the illusion of purity, but has complexity. Why is mixing one so difficult? Because simplicity is difficult thing to achieve. Atomizer sprays, vermouth-flavored ice cubes, vermouth-soaked olives—all have been used to try to reach perfection.

All the ingredients must be chilled—from glasses to gin. Only use the best-quality gin. Be single minded. You are the only person who can make the perfect example.

Martini (Dry)

3 oz. (90 ml/6 tbsp.) chilled dry gin
1 tsp. Noilly Prat
olive or twist of lemon to garnish
There is no more dangerous recipe to write than this—and aficionados should be prepared to be annoyed.

Place the vermouth in shaker with ice. Shake and strain away the excess. Add the gin. Stir and strain into a pre-chilled cocktail glass. Add the lemon twist. Serve. You can vary the amount of vermouth to taste, but the principle remains the same.

L'Amour

2 oz. (60 ml/4 tbsp.) gin
dash cherry brandy
dash grenadine
dash fresh lemon juice
2 sprigs mint
Shake the ingredients, including the mint. Strain into a cocktail glass and serve.

La Bomba

1 oz. (30 ml/2 tbsp.) gold tequila
⅔ oz. (20 ml/1⅓ tbsp.) Cointreau
⅔ oz. (20 ml/1⅓ tbsp.) pineapple juice
⅔ oz. (20 ml/1⅓ tbsp.) fresh orange juice
2 dashes grenadine
Shake the ingredients, then strain into a cocktail glass with a salted rim. Add the grenadine and serve.

La Conga

2 oz. (60 ml/4 tbsp.) silver tequila
2 tsp. pineapple juice
3 dashes Angostura bitters
club soda
lemon slice to garnish
Pour the ingredients, except the soda, into an ice-filled old-fashioned glass. Stir. Fill with soda. Stir. Add the lemon slice and serve.

La Dolce Vita

1 oz. (30 ml/2 tbsp.) vodka
5 seedless grapes
1 tsp. honey
dry sparkling wine (prosecco)
Muddle the grapes in a shaker. Add the vodka and honey and shake. Strain into a champagne flute. Fill with prosecco and serve.

La Floridita

2 oz. (60 ml/4 tbsp.) Havana white rum
dash maraschino liqueur
juice of 1 lime
dash gomme syrup
lime wedge to garnish

**Shake the ingredients with crushed ice, then strain into a cocktail glass
filled with dry crushed ice. Add a lime wedge and serve with a straw.**

Lady Finger

1 oz. (30 ml/2 tbsp.) gin
1 oz. (30 ml/2 tbsp.) cherry brandy
1 oz. (30 ml/2 tbsp.) kirsch

Shake the ingredients, then strain into a martini glass and serve.

Laser Beam

1 oz. (30 ml/2 tbsp.) tequila
1 oz. (30 ml/2 tbsp.) Jack Daniels
1 oz. (30 ml/2 tbsp.) amaretto
½ oz. (15 ml/1 tbsp.) triple sec

Shake the ingredients, then strain into an old-fashioned glass and serve.

Last Gentleman Standing (Metinee Kongsrivilai)

1½ oz (45 ml/3 tbsp.) Speyside malt
½ oz (15 ml/1 tbsp.) Noval Tawny Port
¼ oz (8 ml/½ tbsp.) Green Chartreuse
⅛ oz (5 ml/1 tsp.) morello cherry-infused Maraschino
orange zest and cherry to garnish

Stir and strain into a cocktail glass.
Garnish with orange twist (discard) and a cherry.

Legend

1 oz. (30 ml/2 tbsp.) Midori
1 oz. (30 ml/2 tbsp.) Kahlua
1 oz. (30 ml/2 tbsp.) frangelico
Pour the ingredients into an old-fashioned glass, stir, and serve.

Lemon Drop

1 lemon wedge
1 tsp. sugar
1 oz. (30 ml/2 tbsp.) vodka
**Dip the lemon wedge in the sugar and pour the vodka into a shot glass.
Drink the vodka first, then suck the lemon.**

Liberty Bell

2 oz. (60 ml/4 tbsp.) bourbon
1 oz. (30 ml/2 tbsp.) peach schnapps
dash apricot brandy
dash Campari
**Stir the ingredients in a mixing glass, then strain into a martini glass
and serve.**

Lime Life-Saver (nonalcoholic) (Serves 2)

2 fresh limes
6 medium carrots
knob of ginger
2 fresh apples
**Cut the limes in half and juice. Juice the carrots. Peel the ginger and juice.
Juice the apples. Stir, then pour equally into two tumblers and serve.**

Limey

1 oz. (30 ml/2 tbsp.) lemon vodka
1 oz. (30 ml/2 tbsp.) orange liqueur
1 oz. (30 ml/2 tbsp.) fresh lime juice
Shake the ingredients, then strain into a cocktail glass and serve.

Limp Dick

1 oz. (30 ml/2 tbsp.) Southern Comfort
1 oz. (30 ml/2 tbsp.) Grand Marnier
½ oz. (15 ml/1 tbsp.) amaretto
½ oz. (15 ml/1 tbsp.) white crème de menthe
Stir the ingredients in a glass, then strain into a cocktail glass and serve.

London Cocktail

2 oz. (60 ml/4 tbsp.) London dry gin
dash maraschino liqueur
2 dashes orange bitters
dash gomme syrup
Shake the ingredients, then strain into a cocktail glass and serve.

London Special

2 dashes Angostura bitters
1 twist of orange
chilled champagne
Put the bitters and twist into a flute. Fill with champagne and serve.

Long Island Iced Tea

½ oz. (15 ml/1 tbsp.) light rum
½ oz. (15 ml/1 tbsp.) vodka
½ oz. (15 ml/1 tbsp.) gin
½ oz. (15 ml/1 tbsp.) tequila
½ oz. (15 ml/1 tbsp.) triple sec
juice of 1 lime
cola
Squeeze the lime into a highball, then add ice cubes and the spirits. Stir and fill up with cola. Serve with straws.

Long Island
Iced Tea

Luxury

3 oz. (90 ml/6 tbsp.) cognac
chilled champagne
3 dashes Angostura bitters
Pour the cognac and bitters into a champagne flute, stir, fill with champagne. Stir gently, then serve.

Lychee Martini (see Martini, pp. 104–105)

1 oz. (30 ml/2 tbsp.) vodka
⅓ oz. (10 ml/⅔ tbsp.) lychee liqueur
⅓ oz. (10 ml/⅔ tbsp.) crème de banane
1 oz. (30 ml/2 tbsp.) pineapple juice
Shake the ingredients, then strain into a martini glass and serve.

Made in Cuba (Tom Walker)

2 oz (60 ml/4 tbsp.) Bacardi Superior
1 oz (30 ml/2 tbsp.) lime juice
½ oz (15 ml/1 tbsp.) sugar syrup
handful mint leaves
3 slices cucumber
absinthe rinse
soda
cucumber to garnish
Shake ingredients, double-strain into absinthe-rinsed cocktail glass and top with a splash of soda. Garnish with cucumber slice.

Madras

1½ oz. (45 ml/3 tbsp.) vodka
4 oz. (120 ml/8 tbsp.) cranberry juice
1 oz. (30 ml/2 tbsp.) orange juice
1 wedge of lime
Pour the liquid ingredients into a highball glass over ice. Add the lime wedge and serve.

Madroska

2 oz. (60 ml/4 tbsp.) vodka
3 oz. (90 ml/6 tbsp.) apple juice
2 oz. (60 ml/4 tbsp.) cranberry juice
1 oz. (30 ml/2 tbsp.) fresh orange juice
Pour the ingredients into an ice-filled highball, stir and serve.

Mai Tai No. 1

1 oz. (30 ml/2 tbsp.) white rum
½ oz. (15 ml/1 tbsp.) Cointreau
¼ oz. (8 ml/½ tbsp.) Rose's Lime Cordial
1½ oz. (45 ml/3 tbsp.) orange juice
1½ oz. (45 ml/3 tbsp.) unsweetened
   pineapple juice
splash grenadine
½ oz. (15 ml/1 tbsp.) gold rum
wedge of pineapple to garnish
Shake the ingredients, strain into a highball half-filled with ice. Add the grenadine and gold rum. Garnish and serve.

Mai Tai
No. 1

Mai Tai No. 2

2 oz. (60 ml/4 tbsp.) gold rum
1 oz. (30 ml/2 tbsp.) curaçao
1½ oz. (45 ml/3 tbsp.) Rose's Lime Cordial
½ oz. (15 ml/1 tbsp.) orgeat syrup
1 tsp. gomme syrup
splash grenadine
½ oz. (15 ml/1 tbsp.) overproof rum
wedge of pineapple
wedge of lime to garnish
Shake the ingredients, then strain into a highball glass half-filled with ice. Add the grenadine and overproof rum. Stir. Garnish with the pineapple and lime wedges and serve.

Maiden's Prayer

1 oz. (30 ml/2 tbsp.) gin
½ oz. (15 ml/1 tbsp.) Cointreau
juice of half an orange
juice of half a lemon
Shake the ingredients, then strain into a cocktail glass and serve.

Maiden's Wish

1 oz. (30 ml/2 tbsp.) gin
1 oz. (30 ml/2 tbsp.) Kina Lillet
1 oz. (30 ml/2 tbsp.) calvados
**Stir the ingredients in a mixing glass, then strain into a martini glass
and serve.**

Main Chance

1 oz. (30 ml/2 tbsp.) gin
1 oz. (30 ml/2 tbsp.) triple sec
1 oz. (30 ml/2 tbsp.) fresh grapefruit juice
twist of lime to garnish
**Shake the ingredients, then strain into a cocktail glass. Add the twist
and serve.**

Major Bailey

2 oz. (60 ml/4 tbsp.) gin
dash fresh lime juice
dash fresh lemon juice
1 tsp. granulated sugar
8–10 fresh mint leaves
**Muddle the lime, juices, sugar, and mint in an old-fashioned glass. Add
ice and stir in the gin until the glass is frosted. Serve.**

Mandarine Martini
(see Martini, pp. 104–105)

1½ oz. (45 ml/3 tbsp.) gin
½ oz. (15 ml/1 tbsp.) vodka
splash Mandarine Napoleon
dash Cointreau
twist of mandarin to garnish
**Pour the liqueurs in the shaker. Coat and
discard surplus. Shake the spirits. Strain into
a martini glass. Add the twist and serve.**

Mandarine
Martini

Mango Masher (nonalcoholic)

half a ripe mango
fresh juice of one orange
fresh juice of one lime
handful fresh raspberries
ice cubes
**Take the seeds out of the mango and scoop out the flesh. Cut the citrus
fruit in half and juice them. Put it all in the blender with ice cubes.
Blend until smooth. Pour into a large tumbler and serve.**

Manhattan (see pp. 78–79)

Manhattan (dry) (see Manhattan, pp. 78–79)

2oz. (60 ml/ 4 tbsp) Bourbon or Rye
1 oz. (30 ml/2 tbsp.) dry vermouth
dash Angostura bitters
twist of lemon to garnish
**Half-fill a mixing glass with ice cubes and add the ingredients. Stir, then
strain into a martini glass. Garnish with the lemon and serve.**

Manhattan (Perfect) (see Manhattan, pp. 78–79)

2oz. (60 ml/2 tbsp) Bourbon or Rye
½ oz. (15 ml/1 tbsp) dry vermouth
½ oz. (15 ml/1 tbsp) sweet vermouth
dash Angostura bitters
Half-fill a mixing glass with ice cubes and add the ingredients. Stir, then strain into a martini glass. Garnish with the cherry and serve.

Manhattan (Sweet) (see Manhattan, pp. 78–79)

2 oz. (60 ml/4 tbsp.) bourbon or rye
1 oz. (30 ml/2 tbsp.) sweet vermouth
dash Angostura bitters
maraschino cherry to garnish
Half-fill a mixing glass with ice cubes and pour in all the ingredients. Stir, then strain into a martini glass. Garnish with the cherry and serve.

Margarita (see pp. 92–93)

Martini (Dry) (see pp. 104–105)

Martini Melon (see Martini, pp. 104–105)

1⅔ oz. (50 ml/3⅓ tbsp.) vodka
a quarter of a slice of watermelon
dash fresh lemon juice
Muddle the melon in a shaker. Add ice and the vodka. Shake and strain into a cocktail glass and serve.

Martini Thyme (see Martini, pp. 104–105)

3 oz. (90 ml/6 tbsp.) gin
¾ oz. (22 ml/1½ tbsp.) Green Chartreuse
1 sprig of thyme to garnish
Stir the gin and Chartreuse in a mixing glass. Strain into a martini glass, garnish with the thyme, and serve.

Mary Pickford

1½ oz. (45 ml/3 tbsp.) white rum
dash maraschino liqueur
1½ oz. (45 ml/3 tbsp.)
unsweetened
   pineapple juice dash
grenadinelime twist to garnish
**Shake the ingredients, then strain
into a cocktail glass. Add the twist and serve.**

Matador

2 oz. (60 ml/4 tbsp.) gold tequila
⅔ oz. (20 ml/1⅓ tbsp.) triple sec
juice of 1 lime
5 oz. (150 ml/10 tbsp.) pineapple juice
lime wedge to garnish
**Shake the ingredients, then strain into
an ice-filled highball glass, garnish with a
lime wedge, and serve.**

Matador (alt)

2 oz. (60 ml/4 tbsp.) tequila
¼ oz. (8 ml/½ tbsp.) Cointreau
juice of half a lime
1 tsp. gomme syrup
1 chunk pineapple
**Shake the ingredients with crushed ice,
then strain into a highball glass with a
sugared rim and serve.**

Mary
Pickford

Matador

115

Mayas Daiquiri (David Cordoba)

2 oz (60 ml/4 tbsp.) Bacardi 8YO
¾ oz (22 ml/1½ tbsp.) lime juice
¼ oz (8 ml/½ tbsp.) agave nectar
¼ avocado
pineapple leaf to garnish
Muddle avocado, add all ingredients, shake and double-strain into a cocktail glass. Garnish with pineapple leaf.

Melonball

2 oz. (60 ml/4 tbsp.) Midori melon liqueur
1 oz. (30 ml/2 tbsp.) vodka
pineapple juice
Half-fill a tall glass with ice. Pour in the Midori and vodka. Fill the glass with pineapple juice. Orange juice may also be used.

Melon Margarita (see Margarita, pp. 92–93)

1 oz. (30 ml/2 tbsp.) tequila
⅓ oz. (10 ml/⅔ tbsp.) Cointreau
⅓ oz. (10 ml/⅔ tbsp.) melon liqueur
juice of half a lime
few slices yellow melon, diced
Blend the ingredients. Add crushed ice. Blend, then pour into a margarita glass. Add a straw and serve.

Metropolitan

2 oz. (60 ml/4 tbsp.) blackcurrant vodka
⅔ oz. (20 ml/1⅓ tbsp.) Cointreau
1 oz. (30 ml/2 tbsp.) cranberry juice
dash fresh lime juice
Shake the ingredients, then strain into a cocktail glass and serve.

Metropolitan (alt)

2 oz. (60 ml/4 tbsp.) Absolut Kurant
½ oz. (15 ml/1 tbsp.) Rose's Lime Cordial
½ oz. (15 ml/1 tbsp.) lime juice
1 oz. (30 ml/2 tbsp.) cranberry juice
lime wedge to garnish
Shake the ingredients, then strain into a cocktail glass, garnish with the wedge of lime, and serve.

Mexican Coffee

1 oz. (30 ml/2 tbsp.) Kahlua
6 oz. (180 ml/12 tbsp.) hot black coffee
2 tsp. raw sugar
heavy (double) cream
Pour the Kahlua and black coffee into a liqueur coffee glass, then add the sugar. Float the cream on top and serve.

Mexican Hat

1 oz. (30 ml/2 tbsp.) tequila
1 oz. (30 ml/2 tbsp.) crème de cassis
1 oz. (30 ml/2 tbsp.) champagne
Fill a highball glass three-quarters full with crushed ice, then pour on the tequila, crème de cassis, and lastly, the champagne. Stir carefully and serve.

Mexican Madras

1 oz. (30 ml/2 tbsp.) gold tequila
3 oz. (90 ml/6 tbsp.) cranberry juice
⅔ oz. (20 ml/1⅓ tbsp.) fresh orange juice
dash fresh lime juice
slice of orange to garnish
Shake the ingredients, then strain into an old-fashioned glass filled with ice cubes. Garnish with the slice of orange and serve.

Mint Julep No. 1

"A dram of spirituous liquor that has mint in it, taken by Virginians of a morning."

If Manhattans spark debate, then Mint Juleps can incite war. To crush or not to crush the mint, the quality of the ice, the receptacle, which bourbon to use. All you need are fresh mint, ice, gomme syrup, and bourbon.

If you are one of those Julepians who doesn't believe in bruising the leaves, try gently squeezing the leaves instead or bruise them gently with a muddler in the bottom of the glass. How much mint to use for garnish? Six sprigs are about right. Gary Regan, in his Book of Bourbon, advises cutting the mint at the last minute and allowing some flavor to bleed from the stems into the drink.

A Mint Julep cools you down and freshens you up, making the world a beautiful place. The danger is over-indulgence. Too many, and what should be a soothing Southern experience is turned into something bitter and twisted. The genteel air slips, revealing the decaying, distorted gothic madness that fuels Tennessee Williams, William Faulkner, and the songs of Nick Cave. Then again, some people like that.

Mint Julep No. 1

3 oz. (90 ml/6 tbsp.) bourbon
1 oz. (30 ml/2 tbsp.) simple syrup
3 cups finely crushed ice
6 sprigs of mint

Fill a highball glass two-thirds full with crushed ice. Add the bourbon and syrup. Stir. Pack the glass with more ice so it domes over the top. Garnish with the mint and insert straws. Let stand until a thin layer forms on the glass, then serve.

Mexican Mule

2 oz. (60 ml/4 tbsp.) gold tequila
juice of 1 lime
1 tsp. gomme syrup
ginger ale
Shake the ingredients, then strain into an ice-filled highball. Fill up with ginger ale and serve.

Mexican Runner

1 oz. (30 ml/2 tbsp.) gold tequila
1 oz. (30 ml/2 tbsp.) rum
⅔ oz. (20 ml/1⅓ tbsp.) banana syrup
⅔ oz. (20 ml/1⅓ tbsp.) blackberry syrup
juice of 1 lime
6 strawberries
**Blend the ingredients with crushed ice.
Pour into a tumbler and serve.**

Mexicana

1½ oz. (45 ml/3 tbsp.) tequila
1½ oz. (45 ml/3 tbsp.) unsweetened
pineapple juice
¼ oz. (8 ml/½ tbsp.) fresh lime juice
dash grenadine
**Shake the ingredients, then strain
into an ice-filled highball glass.
Serve with straws.**

Mexicana

Mickey

1 oz. (30 ml/2 tbsp.) dark rum
½ oz. (15 ml/1 tbsp.) Cointreau
½ oz. (15 ml/1 tbsp.) bourbon
dash grenadine
Shake the ingredients, then strain into a martini glass and serve.

Midnight Snowstorm

1 oz. (30 ml/2 tbsp.) white crème de menthe
7 oz. (200 ml/14 tbsp.) hot chocolate
1 oz. (30 ml/2 tbsp.) heavy (double) cream
**Pour the crème de menthe and hot chocolate into a highball glass.
Float the cream on top and serve.**

Mikado

1 oz. (30 ml/2 tbsp.) cognac
½ oz. (15 ml/1 tbsp.) Cointreau
½ oz. (15 ml/1 tbsp.) crème de Noyaux
dash grenadine
**Stir the ingredients, then strain into an ice-filled old-fashioned glass
and serve.**

Mimosa

2 oz. (60 ml/4 tbsp.) fresh orange juice
2 dashes Grand Marnier
champagne
**Fill a champagne flute to a quarter-full with orange juice. Add the Grand
Marnier. Stir. Fill with champagne, stir carefully, and serve.**

Mint Daiquiri (see Daiquiri, pp. 64–65)

2 oz. white rum
½ oz. Cointreau
handful of mint leaves
juice of half a lime
1 tsp. superfine (caster) sugar
**Blend the ingredients with crushed ice, then strain into a cocktail glass
and serve.**

Mint Julep No. 1 (see pp. 118–119)

Mint Julep No. 2 (see Mint Julep, pp. 118–119)

3 oz. (90 ml/6 tbsp.) bourbon
1 oz. (30 ml/2 tbsp.) simple syrup
handful of mint leaves
3 cups freshly finely crushed ice
**Cover the mint leaves with bourbon
for 15 minutes. Take the leaves out
and put in a muslin cloth, then
wring over the bourbon. Put the
fresh bourbon and the syrup in
another bowl. Add the mint "stock"
to taste. Fill a glass with crushed
ice so it domes over the top. Add
the bourbon/mint/syrup mixture.
Add straws and a sprig of mint as
a garnish, then serve.**

Mint Julep
No. 2

Mint Julep (alt) (see Mint Julep, pp. 118–119)

1 oz. (30 ml/2 tbsp.) peach brandy
1 oz. (30 ml/2 tbsp.) brandy
12 sprigs of fresh mint
1 tsp. granulated sugar
chunk of pineapple
**Put the mint in an old-fashioned glass with the sugar and brandies.
Fill the glass with crushed ice and rub the pineapple around the rim.**

Misty

1 oz. (30 ml/2 tbsp.) vodka
1 oz. (30 ml/2 tbsp.) Cointreau
1 oz. (30 ml/2 tbsp.) apricot brandy
dash crème de banane
**Stir the ingredients in a mixing glass, then strain into a martini glass
and serve.**

Mofuco

2 oz. (60 ml/4 tbsp.) white rum
dash Angostura bitters
½ oz. (15 ml/1 tbsp.)
    gomme syrup
1 egg
1 slice lemon peel
Shake the ingredients, then strain into a martini glass and serve.

Mojito

2 oz. (60 ml/4 tbsp.) white rum
1 tsp. gomme syrup
half a lime
fresh mint leaves
soda water
sprig of mint
In a highball glass, muddle the mint leaves and syrup. Squeeze lime juice into the glass and add the lime half. Add the rum, ice, and stir. Add soda water, stir briefly, garnish with the mint, and serve.

Mojito

Molotov Cocktail

3 oz. (90 ml/6 tbsp.) Finlandia vodka
½ oz. (15 ml/1 tbsp.) Black Bush
½ oz. (15 ml/1 tbsp.) Irish Mist
Shake the ingredients, then strain into a cocktail glass and serve.

Molotov
Cocktail

123

Monkey Gland

2 oz. (60 ml/4 tbsp.) gin
1 oz. (30 ml/2 tbsp.) Benedictine
1 oz. (30 ml/2 tbsp.) grenadine
2 oz. (60 ml/4 tbsp.) fresh orange juice
**Shake the ingredients, then strain into a
martini glass and serve.**

Monkey Gland (alt)

2 oz. (60 ml/4 tbsp.) gin
2 oz. (60 ml/4 tbsp.) fresh orange juice
dash absinthe or Pernod
dash grenadine
**Shake the ingredients, then strain into a
cocktail glass and serve.**

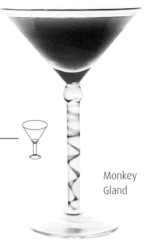

Monkey
Gland

Monte Carlo Highball

2 oz. (60 ml/4 tbsp.) gin
½ oz. (15 ml/1 tbsp.) white crème de menthe
1 oz. (30 ml/2 tbsp.) fresh lemon juice
champagne
**Shake the gin, crème de menthe, and lemon juice, then strain into a
highball glass. Fill up with the champagne and serve.**

Monte Cristo

1 oz. (30 ml/2 tbsp.) Kahlua
1 oz. (30 ml/2 tbsp.) Grand Marnier
6 oz. (180 ml/12 tbsp.) hot black coffee
1 oz. (30 ml/2 tbsp.) heavy (double) cream
**Pour the Kahlua, Grand Marnier, and coffee into a heatproof mug. Float
the cream on top and serve.**

Moscow Mule (see pp. 132–133)

Mother's Milk

1 oz. (30 ml/2 tbsp.) vodka
½ oz. (15 ml/1 tbsp.) gin
½ oz. (15 ml/1 tbsp.) Tia Maria
½ oz. (15 ml/1 tbsp.) orgeat syrup
4 oz. (120 ml/8 tbsp.) milk
Shake the ingredients, then pour into an old-fashioned glass and serve.

Mudslide

2 oz. (60 ml/4 tbsp.) vodka
2 oz. (60 ml/4 tbsp.) Kahlua
2 oz. (60 ml/4 tbsp.) Bailey's Irish cream
Mix with crushed ice in a shaker. Serve in a chilled highball glass.

Mulled Wine

1 bottle claret
4 oz. (120 ml/8 tbsp.) port
rind of 1 lemon
rind of 1 orange
4 tbsp. sugar
10 cloves
2 whole cinnamon sticks
4 oz. (120 ml/8 tbsp.) boiling water
Heat the wine and port with all the other ingredients in a saucepan for a minimum of 15 minutes. Pour individual servings into heatproof glasses. Serve hot.

Multiple Orgasm

1 oz. (30 ml/2 tbsp.) gold tequila
⅔ oz. (20 ml/1⅓ tbsp.) amaretto
⅔ oz. (20 ml/1⅓ tbsp.) coffee liqueur
⅔ oz. (20 ml/1⅓ tbsp.) Irish cream liqueur
1 oz. (30 ml/2 tbsp.) heavy
   (double) cream
2 oz. (60 ml/4 tbsp.) milk
**Shake the ingredients, except the
tequila, strain into an ice-filled highball
glass. Float the tequila on top and serve.**

Naked Lady

1 oz. (30 ml/2 tbsp.) white rum
1 oz. (30 ml/2 tbsp.) apricot brandy
1 oz. (30 ml/2 tbsp.) fresh lemon juice
dash grenadine
1 egg white
**Shake the ingredients, then strain
into a martini glass and serve.**

Naked
Lady

Naked Lady (alt)

1½ oz. (45 ml/3 tbsp.) white rum
1½ oz. (45 ml/3 tbsp.) sweet vermouth
4 dashes apricot brandy
2 dashes grenadine
4 dashes lemon & lime juice
Shake the ingredients, then strain into a martini glass and serve.

Naked Martini (see Martini, pp. 104–105)

2 oz. (60 ml/4 tbsp.) dry gin (at room temperature)
1 olive infused with vermouth
**Pour the gin directly into a martini glass, then add the olive.
Stir and serve.**

Napoleon

2 oz. (60 ml/4 tbsp.) gin
2 dashes orange curaçao
2 dashes Dubonnet
Stir all the ingredients, then strain into a martini glass and serve.

Negroni

1 oz. (30 ml/2 tbsp.) Campari
1 oz. (30 ml/2 tbsp.) sweet vermouth
slice of orange to garnish
splash of soda water (optional)
**Over ice, pour the Campari and sweet
vermouth into an old-fashioned
glass and stir. Add the soda, garnish
with the orange slice, and serve
with straws.**

Negroni (alt)

1½ oz. (45 ml/3 tbsp.) gin
1½ oz. (45 ml/3 tbsp.) Campari
1½ oz. (45 ml/3 tbsp.) sweet vermouth
soda water (optional)
slice of orange to garnish
**Shake the ingredients, then pour over
ice in a highball glass. Fill with soda,
add the garnish, and serve.**

Negroni
(alt)

Neopolitan

2 oz. (60 ml/4 tbsp.) Cointreau
1 oz. (30 ml/2 tbsp.) Grand Marnier
1 oz. (30 ml/2 tbsp.) white rum
Shake the ingredients, then strain into a martini glass and serve.

Nevada

2 oz. (60 ml/4 tbsp.) white rum
1 oz. (30 ml/2 tbsp.) grapefruit juice
juice of 1 lime
Shake the ingredients, then strain into a martini glass and serve.

New England Iced Tea

1 oz. (30 ml/2 tbsp.) vodka
1 oz. (30 ml/2 tbsp.) triple sec
1 oz. (30 ml/2 tbsp.) gold tequila
1 oz. (30 ml/2 tbsp.) light rum
1 oz. (30 ml/2 tbsp.) gin
1 oz. (30 ml/2 tbsp.) fresh lime juice
1 oz. (30 ml/2 tbsp.) gomme syrup
cranberry juice
**Shake the ingredients, except the cranberry juice. Strain into an
ice-filled highball glass. Fill up with cranberry juice and stir. Serve.**

New Orleans Gin Fizz

2 oz. (60 ml/4 tbsp.) gin
1 oz. (30 ml/2 tbsp.) Cointreau
½ oz. (15 ml/1 tbsp.) kirsch
wedge of lemon
2 oz. (60 ml/4 tbsp.) light (single) cream
orange flower water
soda water
**Coat the rim of a tall glass with sugar and half-fill it with ice. Add all
the liquid ingredients except for the orange flower water which can be
used either to coat the glass or as a float on top of the cocktail. Garnish
with the lemon wedge.**

Nineteen

2 oz. (60 ml/4 tbsp.) dry vermouth
½ oz. (15 ml/1 tbsp.) kirsch
½ oz. (15 ml/1 tbsp.) gin
2 dashes Angostura bitters
½ oz. (15 ml/1 tbsp.) gomme syrup
Shake the ingredients, then strain into a martini glass and serve.

North Pole

2 oz. (60 ml/4 tbsp.) gin
1 oz. (30 ml/2 tbsp.) maraschino liqueur
1 oz. (30 ml/2 tbsp.) fresh lemon juice
1 egg white
½ oz. (15 ml/1 tbsp.) heavy (double) cream
Shake the ingredients, except the cream, then strain into a martini glass. Float the cream on top and serve.

Nth Degree (Nate Dumas)

1 oz (30 ml/2 tbsp.) aged rhum agricole
1 oz (30 ml/2 tbsp.) bonded applejack
½ oz (15 ml/1 tbsp.) Green Chartreuse
¼ oz (8 ml/½ tbsp.) Demerara sugar syrup
2 dashes Whiskey Barrel Bitters
lemon and orange peel to garnish
Stir over ice, then strain into an ice-filled rocks glass. Garnish with lemon and orange twist.

Nuptial

2 oz. (60 ml/4 tbsp.) gin
1 oz. (30 ml/2 tbsp.) kirsch
dash Cointreau
dash fresh lemon juice
Shake the ingredients, then strain into a martini glass and serve.

Old-Fashioned

3 oz. (90 ml/6 tbsp.) bourbon
3 dashes Angostura bitters
1 sugar cube
ice cubes
slice of orange
maraschino cherry to garnish

**Put the bitters, sugar cube, and a dash of
the bourbon into an old-fashioned glass and
muddle. Add two ice cubes and 2 tablespoons
of the bourbon and stir. Squeeze some of the
juice from the orange slice into the glass,
then add two more ice cubes and 2 more
tablespoons of the bourbon and stir again.
Finally, add two more ice cubes and the
remaining bourbon. Garnish with the orange
slice and the cherry.**

Old- Fashioned

Old Vermouth

1 oz. (30 ml/2 tbsp.) Old Tom gin
1 oz. (30 ml/2 tbsp.) dry vermouth
½ oz. (15 ml/1 tbsp.) sweet vermouth
2 dashes Angostura bitters
slice of lemon to garnish
**Pour the ingredients into an old-fashioned glass and stir. Garnish with
the lemon slice and serve.**

Olympia

2 oz. (60 ml/4 tbsp.) white rum
½ oz. (15 ml/1 tbsp.) Cherry Heering
juice of 1 lime
Shake the ingredients, then strain into a martini glass and serve.

On a Wave

1 oz. (30 ml/2 tbsp.) gin
1 oz. (30 ml/2 tbsp.) light rum
⅔ oz. (20 ml/1⅓ tbsp.) blue curaçao
3 oz. (90 ml/6 tbsp.) pineapple juice
1 oz. (30 ml/2 tbsp.) fresh lime juice
2 dashes gomme syrup
pineapple wedge to garnish
Shake the ingredients, then strain into a colada glass filled with crushed ice. Garnish with a pineapple wedge and serve.

On the Beach (nonalcoholic)

¼ of a ripe yellow melon, diced
8 raspberries
3 oz. (90 ml/6 tbsp.) fresh orange juice
juice of half a lime
dash grenadine
lemon & lime soda
Blend ingredients for a few seconds, then add a scoop of ice. Blend. Pour into a tumbler and fill with lemon & lime soda. Stir and serve with a straw.

Onion Breath

2 oz. (60 ml/4 tbsp.) vodka
½ oz. (15 ml/1 tbsp.) vinegar from cocktail onions
1 drop Worcestershire sauce
½ oz. (15 ml/1 tbsp.) lemon juice
2 cocktail onions to garnish
Shake the ingredients, then strain into a martini glass. Garnish with the onions and serve.

Moscow Mule

No two words conjure up a more amusing idea than a plodding mule and an effervescent beer.

Back in the 1940s when America hadn't woken up to vodka, John Martin of the drinks import company, Heublein, met in New York with Jack Morgan, the owner of the Cock 'n' Bull restaurant in Hollywood, California. Morgan had landed himself with a surplus of ginger beer, which was proving difficult to shift.

Martin wanted to get rid of the equally slow-moving Smirnoff vodka, for which he'd put his reputation on the line. Morgan and Martin put their heads and their products together, added a splash of lime juice, and created the Moscow Mule.

They then ordered 500 copper mugs engraved with a kicking mule and marketed it to cocktail bars. On the backpack of the mule, Smirnoff vodka's sales tripled between 1947 and 1950, and then doubled again the year after. America would never be the same again. And it's still alive and kickin' as a popular drink, despite the canned and bottled varieties on offer.

Moscow Mule

2 oz. (60 ml/4 tbsp.) vodka
ginger beer
squeeze lime juice
wedge of lime to garnish
**Pour the vodka over ice in
a highball glass. Add the
other ingredients. Stir, add
the garnish, and serve.**

Opal

1⅔ oz. (50 ml/3⅓ tbsp.) gin
⅔ oz. (20 ml/1⅓ tbsp.) Cointreau
1 oz. (30 ml/2 tbsp.) fresh orange juice
twist of orange to garnish
**Shake the ingredients and strain into a cocktail glass. Add the twist
of orange and serve.**

Orange Blossom

2 oz. (60 ml/4 tbsp.) vodka
2 oz. (60 ml/4 tbsp.) orange juice
dash orange flower water
Shake the ingredients, then strain into a cocktail glass and serve.

Orange Blossom Special

1⅔ oz. (50 ml/3⅓ tbsp.) gin
⅔ oz. (20 ml/1⅓ tbsp.) Cointreau
⅔ oz. (20 ml/1⅓ tbsp.) lychee liqueur
⅓ oz. (10 ml/⅔ tbsp.) fresh lemon juice
Shake the ingredients, then strain into a cocktail glass and serve.

Orange Cadillac

1 oz. (30 ml/2 tbsp.) white crème de cacao
1 oz. (30 ml/2 tbsp.) Galliano
½ oz. (15 ml/1 tbsp.) Cointreau
½ oz. (15 ml/1 tbsp.) fresh orange juice
1 oz. (30 ml/2 tbsp.) heavy (double) cream
Shake the ingredients, then strain into a martini glass and serve.

Orange Caipirovska

2 oz. (60 ml/4 tbsp.) orange vodka
⅔ oz. (20 ml/1⅓ tbsp.) fresh lemon juice
half an orange, diced
**Muddle the orange and sugar in an old-fashioned glass. Add the
remaining ingredients. Fill with crushed ice and serve.**

Orchid

2 oz. (60 ml/4 tbsp.) Seager gin
1 oz. (30 ml/2 tbsp.) crème de noyeaux
1 oz. (30 ml/2 tbsp.) lemon juice
½ oz. (15 ml/1 tbsp.) forbidden fruit liqueur
½ oz. (15 ml/1 tbsp.) crème yvette
**Frost the rim of a Cocktail glass with sugar. Shake all the
ingredients and strain into the glass.**

Oriental

1½ oz. (45 ml/3 tbsp.) gin
⅔ oz. (20 ml/1⅓ tbsp.) limoncello
1 oz. (30 ml/2 tbsp.) passion fruit purée
dash passion fruit syrup
twist of lemon to garnish
**Shake the ingredients, then strain into a
cocktail glass. Add a twist of lemon and serve.**

Original Martinez (see Martini, pp. 104–105)

2 oz. (60 ml/4 tbsp.) Old Tom gin
½ oz. (15 ml/1 tbsp.) sweet vermouth
2 dashes maraschino liqueur
dash orange (or lemon) bitters
**Shake the ingredients, then strain into a
martini glass and serve.**

Original
Martinez

Oye Mi Canto (Alex Kratena)

2 oz (60 ml/4 tbsp.) Martini Rosato
1 oz (30 ml/2 tbsp.) Tapatio blanco infused with sweet tamarind
⅛ oz (5 ml/1 tsp.) Mezcal Chichicapa
1 dash orange and mandarin bitters
jasmine flower and apple blossom to garnish
Stir, then strain into a cocktail glass with one ice cube.
Garnish with flowers.

Pacific Gold

1 oz. (30 ml/2 tbsp.) crème de banane
1 oz. (30 ml/2 tbsp.) Cointreau
½ oz. (15 ml/1 tbsp.) Grand Marnier
2 dashes kummel
Stir the ingredients in a mixing glass, then strain into a martini glass and serve.

Painkiller

2 oz. (60 ml/4 tbsp.) white rum
4 oz. (120 ml/8 tbsp.) pineapple juice
1 oz. (30 ml/2 tbsp.) fresh orange juice
1 oz. (30 ml/2 tbsp.) coconut cream
Shake the ingredients, then strain into an ice-filled highball glass and serve.

Pan-Am

1 oz. (30 ml/2 tbsp.) bourbon
1 oz. (30 ml/2 tbsp.) mescal
dash Angostura bitters
dash gomme syrup
Pour the ingredients into an old-fashioned glass, stir, and serve.

Parked Car

1 oz. (30 ml/2 tbsp.) Campari
1 oz. (30 ml/2 tbsp.) tequila
½ oz. (15 ml/1 tbsp.) Cointreau
1 egg white
Shake the ingredients, then strain into a martini glass and serve.

Parson's Nose

2 oz. (60 ml/4 tbsp.) vodka
½ oz. (15 ml/1 tbsp.) amaretto
½ oz. (15 ml/1 tbsp.) crème de peche
dash Angostura bitters
Stir the ingredients in a mixing glass, then strain into a martini glass and serve.

Passion (Chris Edwardes)

1 oz. (30 ml/2 tbsp.) eight-year-old Bacardi
½ oz. (15 ml/1 tbsp.) crème de peche
juice of 1 lime
½ oz. (15 ml/1 tbsp.) gomme syrup
1 oz. (30 ml/2 tbsp.) passion fruit purée
champagne
Shake the ingredients, except the champagne, then strain into an ice-filled highball glass. Fill with champagne and serve.

Passion Batida

1⅔ oz. (50 ml/3⅓ tbsp.) cachaça
1 oz. (30 ml/2 tbsp.) passion fruit purée
⅓ oz. (10 ml/⅔ tbsp.) gomme syrup
lime wedge to garnish
Pour the ingredients into an ice-filled old-fashioned glass. Stir and garnish with a lime wedge.

Peach Cocktail

2 oz. (60 ml/4 tbsp.) crème de peche
1 oz. (30 ml/2 tbsp.) dry vermouth
dash grenadine
Shake the ingredients, then strain into a martini glass and serve.

Peach Margarita (see Margarita, pp. 92–93)

1 oz. (30 ml/2 tbsp.) silver tequila
½ oz. (15 ml/1 tbsp.) Cointreau
½ oz. (15 ml/1 tbsp.) peach schnapps
juice of half a lime
1 peach, peeled and diced
Blend the peach pieces, then add the other ingredients. Blend. Pour into a margarita glass and serve.

Pear Daiquiri (see Daiquiri, pp. 64–65)

1 oz. (30 ml/2 tbsp.) white rum
⅓ oz. (10 ml/⅔ tbsp.) pear schnapps
1 oz. (30 ml/2 tbsp.) fresh pear purée
1 oz. (30 ml/2 tbsp.) fresh lime juice
dash gomme syrup
Blend the ingredients with crushed ice. Pour into a large cocktail glass and serve.

Penicillin (Sam Ross)

2 oz (60 ml/4 tbsp.) blended Scotch
¾ oz (22 ml/1½ tbsp.) lemon juice
⅛ oz (5 ml/1 tsp.) honey syrup
½ oz (15 ml/1 tbsp.) sweetened ginger juice
¼ oz (8 ml/½ tbsp.) Islay Scotch float
candied ginger to garnish
Shake all except float, then strain over ice in a rocks glass. Garnish with candied ginger.

Pearl Harbor

1 oz. (30 ml/2 tbsp.) vodka
⅔ oz. (20 ml/1 tbsp.) melon liqueur
1 oz. (30 ml/2 tbsp.) pineapple juice
Shake the ingredients, then strain into a cocktail glass and serve.

Pernod Cocktail

2 oz. (60 ml/4 tbsp.) Pernod
2 oz. (60 ml/4 tbsp.) iced water
2 dashes Angostura bitters
Pour the Pernod, water, and the bitters into an old-fashioned glass and serve.

Pierre Collins

2 oz. (60 ml/4 tbsp.) cognac
1 oz. (30 ml/2 tbsp.) lemon juice
1 tsp. superfine (caster) sugar
dash Angostura bitters (optional)
soda
Place the first three ingredients in a highball glass half-filled with ice and stir to mix. Fill up with soda. Stir gently and serve.

Pierre Fizz

2 oz. (60 ml/4 tbsp.) cognac
1 oz. (30 ml/2 tbsp.) lemon juice
1 tsp. superfine (caster) sugar
dash Angostura bitters (optional)
soda
Shake the ingredients, then strain into a highball glass, fill up with soda, and serve.

Pimm's Royal

1 oz. (30 ml/2 tbsp.) Pimm's
5 oz. (150 ml/10 tbsp.) champagne
**Pour the Pimm's and champagne into a
champagne flute, stir, then serve.**

Pina Colada

2 oz. (60 ml/4 tbsp.) white rum
1 oz. (30 ml/2 tbsp.) sweetened
    coconut cream
2 oz. (60 ml/4 tbsp.) pineapple juice
4 chunks fresh pineapple
pinch of salt
**Blend the ingredients until smooth,
then pour into a colada glass and
serve with straws.**

Pina
Colada

Pine Smoothie (nonalcoholic)

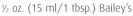

quarter of a large fresh pineapple
juice of one orange
2 handfuls raspberries
ice cubes
**Peel the pineapple and dice the flesh. Blend with the orange juice
and berries. Add the ice cubes last. Blend and pour into a tumbler
and serve.**

Pineapple Upside-Down Cake

½ oz. (15 ml/1 tbsp.) Bailey's
½ oz. (15 ml/1 tbsp.) vodka
½ oz. (15 ml/1 tbsp.) butterscotch schnapps
½ oz. (15 ml/1 tbsp.) pineapple juice
**Stir the ingredients in a mixing glass, then strain into a shot glass
and serve.**

Pink Awakening (nonalcoholic) (Makes 2 glasses)

2 large handfuls raspberries
ripe banana
fresh juice of one pink grapefruit
**Rinse the raspberries and place in a blender. Add the peeled banana
and grapefruit juice. Blend, pour into a tumbler, and serve.**

Pink Caddie-O

1 oz. (30 ml/2 tbsp.) gold tequila
⅔ oz. (20 ml/1⅓ tbsp.) Grand Marnier
1 oz. (30 ml/2 tbsp.) cranberry juice
fresh juice of 1 lime
Shake the ingredients, then strain into a cocktail glass and serve.

Pink Cadillac

1 oz. (30 ml/2 tbsp.) crème de cacao
½ oz. (15 ml/1 tbsp.) Galliano
½ oz. (15 ml/1 tbsp.) grenadine
1 oz. (30 ml/2 tbsp.) heavy (double) cream
dash fresh orange juice
Shake the ingredients, then strain into a martini glass and serve.

Pink Fetish

1 oz. (30 ml/2 tbsp.) vodka
1 oz. (30 ml/2 tbsp.) peach schnapps
2 oz. (60 ml/4 tbsp.) cranberry juice
2 oz. (60 ml/4 tbsp.) fresh orange juice
lime wedge to garnish
**Shake the ingredients, then strain into an ice-filled old-fashioned glass.
Add a lime wedge and serve.**

Pink Gin

4 oz. (120 ml/8 tbsp.) gin
2 dashes Angostura bitters
Coat a chilled cocktail glass with the Angostura bitters. Discard the excess, fill up with the gin, and serve.

Pink Lady

1 oz. (30 ml/2 tbsp.) gin
2 dashes grenadine
one egg white
juice of half a lemon
Shake the ingredients, then strain into a martini glass and serve.

Pink Gin

Pink Rose

2 oz. (60 ml/4 tbsp.) gin
½ oz. (15 ml/1 tbsp.) light (single) cream
½ oz. (15 ml/1 tbsp.) fresh orange juice
2 dashes grenadine
one egg white
Shake the ingredients, then strain into a martini glass and serve.

Pisco Sour (see pp. 146–147)

Planter's

2 oz. (60 ml/4 tbsp.) dark rum
juice of 1 lime
½ oz. (15 ml/1 tbsp.) gomme syrup
Shake the ingredients, then strain into a martini glass and serve.

Poinsettia

1 oz. (30 ml/2 tbsp.) Cointreau
chilled champagne
twist of orange to garnish
**Pour the Cointreau and champagne into a champagne flute.
Stir, add the garnish, and serve.**

Polish Martini (see Martini, pp. 104–105)

1½ oz. (45 ml/3 tbsp.) Wyborowa vodka
½ oz. (15 ml/1 tbsp.) Krupnik vodka
dash apple juice
Shake the ingredients, then strain into a martini glass and serve.

Prado

1 oz. (30 ml/2 tbsp.) tequila
2 tsp. maraschino liqueur
juice of 1 lime
2 dashes grenadine
1 tsp. egg white powder
maraschino cherry and slice of lime to garnish
**Shake the ingredients, then strain into an ice-filled old-fashioned glass.
Add the maraschino cherry and slice of lime and serve.**

Prairie Oyster (nonalcoholic)

1 tsp. olive oil
3 dashes Worcestershire sauce
1 egg yolk
salt
black pepper
1 oz. (30 ml/2 tbsp.) tomato ketchup
dash white wine vinegar
**Rinse a wine glass with the olive oil and discard the oil. Add the tomato
ketchup and egg yolk. Season with Worcestershire sauce, wine vinegar,
and salt and pepper. Serve with a small glass of iced water on the side.**

President

2 oz. (60 ml/4 tbsp.) dark rum
dash grenadine
juice of half a ruby orange
dash lemon juice
Shake the ingredients, then strain into a martini glass and serve.

Presidente

2 oz. (60 ml/4 tbsp.) white rum
¼ oz. (8 ml/½ tbsp.) Cointreau
¾ oz. (22 ml/1½ tbsp.) dry vermouth
¼ oz. (8 ml/½ tbsp.) sweet vermouth
dash grenadine
dash lime juice

Presidente

Shake the ingredients, then strain into a cocktail glass and serve.

Prince of Wales

¾ oz. (22 ml/1½ tbsp.) brandy
¼ oz. (8 ml/½ tbsp.) Benedictine
champagne
dash of Angostura bitters
1 sugar cube
slice of orange to garnish
cherry to garnish
Place the sugar cube in a highball glass and soak it with the Angostura. Add the ice, brandy, and fruit. Stir, then add the champagne. Finally, add the Benedictine, garnish, and serve.

Purple Hooter

1 oz. (30 ml/2 tbsp.) citrus vodka
½ oz. (15 ml/1 tbsp.) triple sec
½ oz. (15 ml/1 tbsp.) Chambord
Shake the ingredients, then strain into a shot glass and serve.

Pussy Foot

2 oz. (60 ml/4 tbsp.) white rum
1 oz. (30 ml/2 tbsp.) fresh lime juice
1 oz. (30 ml/2 tbsp.) fresh orange juice
1 oz. (30 ml/2 tbsp.) pineapple juice
2 dashes grenadine
1 oz. (30 ml/2 tbsp.) heavy (double) cream
Shake the ingredients, then strain into a highball glass and serve.

Queen Elizabeth

2 oz. (60 ml/4 tbsp.) gin
1 oz. (30 ml/2 tbsp.) dry vermouth
½ oz. (15 ml/1 tbsp.) Benedictine
Stir the gin, vermouth, and Benedictine in a mixing glass, then strain into a martini glass and serve.

Quiet Rage

1⅔ oz. (50 ml/3⅓ tbsp.) vodka
2 oz. (60 ml/4 tbsp.) guava juice
2 oz. (60 ml/4 tbsp.) pineapple juice
4 fresh lychees
1 oz. (30 ml/2 tbsp.) coconut cream
dash grenadine
Blend the ingredients with crushed ice. Pour into a highball glass and serve.

Pisco Sour

One or two lead to three or four and you might
end up behaving like the Pisco Kid!

Sours are one of the great workhorses of the cocktail bar. Any
spirit can be combined with lemon juice and sugar to make a
mouth-puckering drink. The Pisco Sour is exceptional, and it is the
national drink of Chile and Peru, sipped as a cooling drink during
the hot South American summers.

It's easy to drink, thanks to the aromatic, apparently benign
influence of the Pisco. So, you have another—and another. All of a
sudden, this gentle drink turns around and belts you on the back
of the neck, distorting your vision. You might feel an
overwhelming urge to dance like a crazy fool. Be warned, once
Pisco madness is unleashed it is difficult to keep under control.

Use a top brand, and go for the top designation of Gran Pisco. This
is the driest and most flavorsome—and flavor is the whole point
of the exercise. Most arguments revolve around whether to use
egg whites or not. Pisco Sour experts prefer to keep them away.
Bitters are also used by some, although they can be a touch
abrasive. If you must, try to find and use orange or Peychaud
bitters rather than Angostura bitters.

Pisco Sour

2 oz. (60 ml/4 tbsp.) Gran Pisco
1 oz. (30 ml/2 tbsp.) lemon juice
1 tsp. superfine (caster) sugar
egg white (optional)
bitters (optional)
Shake the ingredients well, particularly if you are using an egg white, then strain into an old-fashioned glass and serve.

Raja

1 oz. (30 ml/2 tbsp.) cognac
1 oz. (30 ml/2 tbsp.) champagne
Stir the cognac and champagne in a mixing glass, then strain into a martini glass and serve.

Rapscallion (Adeline Shepherd and Craig Harper)

2¼ oz (68 ml/4½ tbsp.) Talisker 10YO whisky
¾ oz (22 ml/1½ tbsp.) PX sherry
Absinthe rinse
lemon twist to garnish
Stir and strain into absinthe-rinsed cocktail glass. Garnish with lemon twist (discard).

Raspberry Collins

2 oz. (60 ml/4 tbsp.) gin
⅔ oz. (20 ml/1⅓ tbsp.) crème de framboise
1⅔ oz. (50 ml/3⅓ tbsp.) fresh lemon juice
⅓ oz. (10 ml/⅔ tbsp.) gomme syrup
3 oz. (90 ml/6 tbsp.) raspberry purée
club soda
3 raspberries to garnish
Shake the ingredients, except the soda. Strain into a highball. Fill with soda. Add the raspberries on a cocktail stick and serve.

Raspberry Mint Daiquiri (see Daiquiri, pp. 64–65)

1⅔ oz. (50 ml/3⅓ tbsp.) white rum
handful fresh raspberries
6 mint leaves
Shake the ingredients, then strain into a large cocktail glass.

Raspberry Martini (see Martini, pp. 104–105)

2 oz. (60 ml/4 tbsp.) vodka
1 oz. (30 ml/2 tbsp.) crème de framboise
10 raspberries
Muddle the raspberries in a shaker. Add the vodka and crème de framboise. Shake, then strain into a martini glass and serve.

Raspberry Sip

1 oz. (30 ml/2 tbsp.) fresh raspberry juice
½ oz. (15 ml/1 tbsp.) Cointreau
½ oz. (15 ml/1 tbsp.) crème de banane
champagne
Shake the ingredients, except the champagne, then strain the mixture into a champagne flute. Fill with champagne, stir, and serve.

Red Russian

1 oz. (30 ml/2 tbsp.) vodka
1 oz. (30 ml/2 tbsp.) white crème de cacao
2 dashes grenadine
Shake the ingredients, then strain into an ice-filled old-fashioned glass and serve.

Ritz Fizz

dash amaretto
dash blue curaçao
dash fresh lemon juice
chilled champagne
Pour the first three ingredients into a champagne flute, stir, then fill with champagne and serve.

Road Runner

1 oz. (30 ml/2 tbsp.) vodka
⅔ oz. (20 ml/1⅓ tbsp.) amaretto
⅔ oz. (20 ml/1⅓ tbsp.) coconut cream
Shake the ingredients, then strain into a martini glass and serve.

Rob Roy

2 oz. (60 ml/4 tbsp.) Scotch whisky
1 oz. (30 ml/2 tbsp.) sweet vermouth
dash Angostura bitters
Stir the scotch, vermouth, and bitters in a mixing glass, then strain into a martini glass and serve.

Rob Roy Perfect

2 oz. (60 ml/4 tbsp.) Scotch whisky
½ oz. (15 ml/1 tbsp.) sweet vermouth
½ oz. (15 ml/1 tbsp.) dry vermouth
dash Angostura bitters
Stir the ingredients in a mixing glass, then strain into a cocktail glass and serve.

Ronaldo

1 oz. (30 ml/2 tbsp.) cachaça
1 oz. (30 ml/2 tbsp.) gold rum
½ oz. (15 ml/1 tbsp.) crème de banane
½ oz. (15 ml/1 tbsp.) unsweetened pineapple juice
dash lime juice
lime wedge to garnish
Shake the ingredients, then strain into a highball glass half-filled with ice. Garnish with the lime wedge and serve.

Rosalita

¾ oz. (22 ml/1½ tbsp.) tequila
¼ oz. (8 ml/½ tbsp.) dry vermouth
¼ oz. (8 ml/½ tbsp.) sweet vermouth
¼ oz. (8 ml/½ tbsp.) Campari
Shake the ingredients, then strain into a cocktail glass and serve.

Royal Blush

1 oz. (30 ml/2 tbsp.) vodka
1 oz. (30 ml/2 tbsp.) crème de framboise
1 oz. (30 ml/2 tbsp.) heavy (double) cream
2 dashes grenadine
Shake the ingredients, then strain into a martini glass and serve.

Rude Cosmopolitan

2 oz. (60 ml/4 tbsp.) gold tequila
⅔ oz. (20 ml/1⅓ tbsp.) triple sec
1 oz. (30 ml/2 tbsp.) cranberry juice
juice of half a lime
twist of orange to garnish
Shake the ingredients, then strain into a cocktail glass. Add the orange twist and serve.

Rum 'n' Coke Float (Ryan Chetiyawardana)

1½ oz (45 ml/3 tbsp.) aged rum
⅗ oz (18 ml/1⅕ tbsp.) Coca-Cola syrup
1 whole egg
lime twist to garnish
Dry-shake all ingredients without ice. Shake with ice, then double-strain into a contour glass. Garnish with lime twist.

Rum Punch

Rum punches are equally open to interpretation. On every island in the Caribbean, every bar will have its own variation, but all will be mixing sour, sweet, strong, and weak components. Sourness is given by lime juice and bitters, sweetness from fruit juices, syrup, and grenadine. Rum is the sole alcohol and most recipes dilute the punch with either water or ice. The end result is a gentle, soothing drink, not some confected mess. In Jamaica, Wray & Nephew dilutes lime, grenadine/syrup, and overproof rum with water, and adds dashes of bitters and nutmeg. In Haiti, they combine orange and passion fruit juice for sweetness and use crushed ice to dilute.

Rum Shrub

2 oz. (60 ml/4 tbsp.) dark rum
1 oz. (30 ml/2 tbsp.) shrub (fruit and herb syrup)
1 oz. (30 ml/2 tbsp.) soda
Fill wine goblet two-thirds with ice. Add the rum, shrub, and soda. Stir lightly and serve.

Russian Bear

1 oz. (30 ml/2 tbsp.) vodka
1½ oz. (45 ml/3 tbsp.) light (single) cream
¼ oz. (8 ml/½ tbsp.) crème de cacao
1 tsp. sugar
Shake the ingredients, then strain into a champagne flute or a cocktail glass and serve.

Russian Bear

Russian Cocktail

1 oz. (30 ml/2 tbsp.) vodka
1 oz. (30 ml/2 tbsp.) gin
1 oz. (30 ml/2 tbsp.) white crème de cacao
**Shake the ingredients, then strain
into a martini glass and serve.**

Russian Coffee

1 oz. (30 ml/2 tbsp.) vodka
6 oz. (180 ml/12 tbsp.) hot black
coffee
2 tsp. raw sugar
heavy (double) cream
**Pour the vodka and black coffee into a
liqueur coffee glass, then add the sugar.
Float the cream on top and serve.**

Rusty Nail

Rusty Nail

2 oz. (60 ml/4 tbsp.) Scotch whisky
1 oz. (30 ml/2 tbsp.) Drambuie
**Pour the scotch and Drambuie
into an old-fashioned glass and
serve with a stirrer.**

Salty Dog

2 oz. (60 ml/4 tbsp.) vodka
2 oz. (60 ml/4 tbsp.) grapefruit juice
**Shake the vodka with the grapefruit juice,
then strain into a champagne
flute or a martini glass and serve.**

Salty Dog

Sangrita
(nonalcoholic) (Serves 10)

35 oz. (1 L/4½ cups) tomato juice
16 oz. (450 ml/2 cups) orange juice
5 tsp. honey
3 oz. (90 ml/6 tbsp.) lime juice
pinch salt and black pepper
1 chili, finely chopped
¼ oz. white onion, finely chopped
10 to 20 dashes Worcestershire sauce
Pour the ingredients into a bowl. Stir well. Place in the refrigerator to chill for two hours. Take out, then strain into a large glass jug. Serve in individual wine glasses.

Sazerac

2½ oz. (75 ml/5 tbsp.) bourbon
2 tsp. absinthe or Pernod
½ tsp. gomme syrup
3 dashes Peychaud's bitters
twist of lemon to garnish
Pour the absinthe/Pernod into a highball glass, coat, and discard the excess. Shake the other ingredients and pour over ice into the glass, then serve.

Scandinavian Coffee

1 oz. (30 ml/2 tbsp.) akvavit
6 oz. (180 ml/12 tbsp.) hot black coffee
2 tsp. raw sugar
heavy (double) cream
Pour the akvavit and black coffee into a liqueur coffee glass, then add the sugar. Float the cream on top and serve.

Scarborough Fair

2 oz. (60 ml/4 tbsp.) Plymouth gin
¼ oz. (8 ml/½ tbsp.) Chambery
sprig of thyme
sprig of rosemary
sprig of flat leaf parsley
2 fresh sage leaves
Muddle the sage, parsley, and Chambery in a shaker. Add the gin. Shake, then strain into a cocktail glass. Garnish with rosemary and thyme leaves and serve.

Screwdriver

2 oz. (60 ml/4 tbsp.) vodka
5 oz. (145 ml/10 tbsp.) fresh orange juice
Pour the vodka into an ice-filled high-ball glass. Add the orange juice, stir, and serve with a stirrer.

Sea Breeze

2 oz. (60 ml/4 tbsp.) vodka
3 oz. (90 ml/6 tbsp.) cranberry juice
2 oz. (60 ml/4 tbsp.) grapefruit juice
Pour the ingredients into an ice-filled highball glass. Stir, then serve with a stirrer and straws.

Sea Breeze

Second Secret (Paul Graham)

1 oz (30 ml/2 tbsp.) rye
1 oz (30 ml/2 tbsp.) bonded applejack
1 oz (30 ml/2 tbsp.) lemon juice
½ oz (15 ml/1 tbsp.) grenadine
lemon twist to garnish
Shake and double-strain into a cocktail glass. Garnish with lemon twist.

Seelbach Cocktail

1 oz. (30 ml/2 tbsp.) Old Forester bourbon
½ oz. (15 ml/1 tbsp.) Cointreau
7 dashes Angostura bitters
7 dashes Peychaud orange bitters
5 oz. (120 ml/10 tbsp.) champagne
twist of orange to garnish
**Pour the bourbon, Cointreau, and both
bitters into a champagne flute and stir.
Add the champagne, stir, garnish with
the twist of orange, and serve.**

September Morn

2 oz. (60 ml/4 tbsp.) white rum
splash grenadine
1 oz. (30 ml/2 tbsp.) lemon juice
1 egg white
**Shake the ingredients for about 30 seconds,
then strain into a cocktail glass and serve.**

Sex on the Beach

½ oz. (15 ml/1 tbsp.) chambord
½ oz. (15 ml/1 tbsp.) midori
½ oz. (15 ml/1 tbsp.) vodka
1 oz. (30 ml/2 tbsp.) pineapple juice
cranberry juice

September
Morn

**Stir the ingredients in a mixing glass, then
strain into a shot glass. Fill up with the
cranberry juice and serve.**

Shirley Temple (nonalcoholic)

7 oz. (200 ml/14 tbsp.) ginger ale
1 oz. (30 ml/2 tbsp.) grenadine syrup
Lemon slice to garnish
Cherry to garnish
Build a pile of ice in a highball glass. Add ginger ale over the ice and sprinkle with grenadine syrup. Garnish with a lemon slice and a cherry.

Short Fuse

2 oz. (60 ml/4 tbsp.) gold tequila
⅔ oz. (20 ml/1⅓ tbsp.) apricot brandy
2 tsp. juice of maraschino cherries
juice of 1 lime
3 oz. (90 ml/6 tbsp.) grapefruit juice
lime wedge to garnish
Shake the ingredients, then strain into an ice-filled highball glass. Add the lime wedge and serve.

Showtime

1 oz. (30 ml/2 tbsp.) gin
⅔ oz. (20 ml/1⅓ tbsp.) lychee liqueur
⅔ oz. (20 ml/1⅓ tbsp.) pineapple liqueur
⅔ oz. (20 ml/1⅓ tbsp.) fresh peach purée
peach slice to garnish
Shake the ingredients, strain into a cocktail glass, add peach slice, and serve.

Sidecar (see pp. 160–161)

Sidecar (alt) (see Sidecar, pp. 160–161)

1½ oz. (45 ml/3 tbsp.) cognac
¾ oz. (22 ml/1½ tbsp.) Cointreau
¾ oz. (22 ml/1½ tbsp.) lemon juice
twist of lemon to garnish
Sugar the rim of a cocktail glass. Shake the ingredients, then strain into the glass, garnish with the twist of lemon, and serve.

Sidney

2 oz. (60 ml/4 tbsp.) rye or bourbon
½ oz. (15 ml/1 tbsp.) dry vermouth
1 splash yellow Chartreuse
dash orange bitters
twist of lemon to garnish
Stir the ingredients in a mixing glass, then strain into a cocktail glass. Add the lemon twist and serve.

Silk Stocking

1 oz. (30 ml/2 tbsp.) tequila
1 oz. (30 ml/2 tbsp.) white crème de cacao
1 oz. (30 ml/2 tbsp.) heavy (double) cream
dash grenadine
Shake the ingredients, then strain into a martini glass and serve.

Silver Bronx

2 oz. (60 ml/4 tbsp.) dry gin
1 oz. (30 ml/2 tbsp.) sweet vermouth
1 oz. (30 ml/2 tbsp.) fresh orange juice
half an egg white
Shake the ingredients, then strain into a champagne flute or a cocktail glass and serve.

Silver
Bronx

Silver Bullet

2 oz. (60 ml/4 tbsp.) vodka
1 oz. (30 ml/2 tbsp.) kummel
Pour the ingredients into an old-fashioned glass, stir, and serve.

Singapore Sling (see pp. 170–171)

Silver Streak

2 oz. (60 ml/4 tbsp.) gin
1 oz. (30 ml/2 tbsp.) kummel
Pour the ingredients into an old-fashioned glass, stir, and serve.

Singapore Gin Sling (see Singapore Sling pp. 170–171)

2 oz. (60 ml/4 tbsp.) gin
½ oz. (15 ml/1 tbsp.) Cointreau
1½ oz. (45 ml/3 tbsp.) fresh lime juice
1 tsp. superfine (caster) sugar
1 tsp. gomme syrup
soda water
¾ oz. (22 ml/1½ tbsp.) Cherry Heering
lime wedge to garnish
Shake the first five ingredients, then strain into a highball glass. Fill up with soda and float the Cherry Heering over the top. Garnish with the lime and serve.

Slow Seducer

½ oz. (15 ml/1 tbsp.) crème de framboise
½ oz. (15 ml/1 tbsp.) Cointreau
1 oz. (30 ml/2 tbsp.) pink grapefruit juice
champagne
Shake the ingredients, except the champagne, then strain into a champagne flute. Fill with champagne, stir, and serve.

Slowly Does It

1 oz. (30 ml/2 tbsp.) tequila
⅔ oz. (20 ml/1⅓ tbsp.) dark rum
2 dashes Tia Maria
1 oz. (30 ml/2 tbsp.) coconut cream
half a banana
2 oz. (60 ml/4 tbsp.) pineapple juice
Blend the ingredients, except the dark rum, with crushed ice. Pour into a tumbler. Float the dark rum on top and serve with a straw.

Sidecar

A classic with a minimalist beauty, perhaps the spiritual father of the Pisco Sour and the Daiquiri.

There are plenty of theories when it comes to naming the person who first made this cocktail. What's beyond doubt is that it is a Parisian creation, but trying to find out who was the first to put cognac, Cointreau, and lemon juice together ends up with you following clues that only lead you up some blind alley in an obscure arrondissement. It is generally thought it was created for a military chap in Paris during the First World War, who used to arrive at Harry's New York Bar, located in a small side street off a main boulevard, in a chauffeur-driven motorcycle sidecar.

It qualifies as a classic for the simple reason that it's a cocktail that has a minimalist beauty—it is, after all, a sour and as such a relative of the Pisco Sour, the Whisky Sour and the Margarita. The important element is to get the correct balance between the mouth-puckering acidity of fresh lemon juice (lime won't do, which is why a Sidecar isn't just a Daiquiri made with brandy) and the clean, sweet, orange richness of triple sec. If these sweet and sour elements are in balance, they provide the ideal frame for the fruity richness and kick of the Cognac.

Sidecar

1 oz. (30 ml/2 tbsp.) brandy
⅔ oz. (20 ml/1⅓ tbsp.) Cointreau
⅔ oz. (20 ml/1⅓ tbsp.) fresh lemon juice
**Shake the ingredients, then strain into
a cocktail glass and serve.**

Smoky Martini (see Martini, pp. 104–105)

2 oz. (60 ml/4 tbsp.) gin
¼ oz. (8 ml/½ tbsp.) Scotch whisky
½ tsp. dry vermouth
Shake the ingredients, then strain into a cocktail glass and serve.

Snow Bunny

1 oz. (30 ml/2 tbsp.) triple sec
6 oz. (180 ml/12 tbsp.) hot chocolate
1 cinnamon stick to garnish
Pour the triple sec into a heatproof glass and fill with the hot chocolate. Garnish with the cinnamon stick and serve.

Soixante-Neuf

1 oz. (30 ml/2 tbsp.) gin
1 oz. (30 ml/2 tbsp.) fresh lemon juice
chilled champagne
twist of lemon to garnish
Shake the gin and lemon juice, then strain into a champagne flute. Fill with champagne, add the twist, and serve.

South of the Border

South of
the Border

1 oz. (30 ml/2 tbsp.) tequila
¾ oz. (22 ml/1½ tbsp.) Kahlua
half a lime
Squeeze the lime over ice in an old-fashioned glass. Stir, then add the spirits. Stir and serve.

Southern Bull

1 oz. (30 ml/2 tbsp.) Kahlua
1 oz. (30 ml/2 tbsp.) Southern Comfort
1 oz. (30 ml/2 tbsp.) tequila
Shake the ingredients, then strain into a martini glass and serve.

Spanish Fly

2 oz. (60 ml/4 tbsp.) mescal
1 oz. (30 ml/2 tbsp.) Grand Marnier
1 tsp. instant coffee to garnish
**Pour the mescal and Grand Marnier into an old-fashioned glass.
Sprinkle with the coffee and serve.**

Spice Whirl

1 oz. (30 ml/2 tbsp.) spiced rum
⅔ oz. (20 ml/1⅓ tbsp.) triple sec
1 oz. (30 ml/2 tbsp.) fresh orange juice
1 oz. (30 ml/2 tbsp.) papaya juice
⅔ oz. (20 ml/1⅓ tbsp.) fresh lime juice
**Shake the ingredients, then strain into an ice-filled highball.
Serve with a straw.**

Star

1 oz. (30 ml/2 tbsp.) dry gin
1 oz. (30 ml/2 tbsp.) calvados
dash Noilly Prat
dash dry vermouth
dash grapefruit juice
**Stir the ingredients in a mixing glass, then strain
into a cocktail glass and serve.**

Stinger

2 oz. (60 ml/4 tbsp.) brandy
1 oz. (30 ml/2 tbsp.) white crème de menthe
**Pour the brandy and crème de menthe into a brandy
glass, stir, and serve. Alternatively, shake the
ingredients, then strain into a martini or old-
fashioned glass.**

Stinger

Straits Sling (see Singapore Sling, pp. 170–171)

2 oz. (60 ml/4 tbsp.) Beefeater gin
2 oz. (60 ml/4 tbsp.) fresh lime juice
½ oz. (15 ml/1 tbsp.) Benedictine
½ oz. (15 ml/1 tbsp.) Peter Heering
2 tsp. sugar
dash of Angostura Bitters
**Pour the gin, lime juice, and bitters
over crushed ice in a highball glass.
Add the sugar and stir. Then add
the Benedictine and Peter Heering,
fill up with soda, and serve.**

Strawberry Cream Tea

1 oz. (30 ml/2 tbsp.) Kahlua
1 oz. (30 ml/2 tbsp.) Bailey's
1 oz. (30 ml/2 tbsp.) fraise
1 oz. (30 ml/2 tbsp.) vodka
1 oz. (30 ml/2 tbsp.) lassi (Indian
   yogurt drink)
strawberry to garnish
**Blend the ingredients, then pour into an
ice-filled highball glass. Serve with a
strawberry on the rim. Lassi gives this
cocktail a lighter, cleaner flavor.**

Strawberry
Cream Tea

Strawberry Daiquiri (see Daiquirii, pp. 64–65)

½ oz. (15 ml/1 tbsp.) strawberry schnapps
1 oz. (30 ml/2 tbsp.) light rum
1 oz. (30 ml/2 tbsp.) lime juice
1 oz. (30 ml/2 tbsp.) powdered sugar
1 oz. (25 g) strawberries, pulped
Shake all ingredients with ice, strain into a cocktail glass, and serve.

Superior

2 oz. (60 ml/4 tbsp.) white rum
1 oz. (30 ml/2 tbsp.) sweet vermouth
1 oz. (30 ml/2 tbsp.) fresh lemon juice
2 fresh apricots
slice of orange to garnish
**Blend the ingredients until frozen, then pour into a large goblet.
Garnish with the orange slice and serve.**

Swamp Water

1 oz. (30 ml/2 tbsp.) green crème de menthe
1 oz. (30 ml/2 tbsp.) Bailey's
1 oz. (30 ml/2 tbsp.) cherry brandy
Pour the ingredients into an ice-filled brandy glass, stir, and serve.

Swan Song

1 oz. (30 ml/2 tbsp.) midori
½ oz. (15 ml/1 tbsp.) Cointreau
½ oz. (15 ml/1 tbsp.) frangelico
grated chocolate to garnish
**Shake the ingredients, then strain into a cocktail glass. Sprinkle with
the chocolate and serve.**

Sydney Sling (see Singapore Sling, pp. 170–171)

2 oz. (60 ml/4 tbsp.) white rum
⅔ oz. (20 ml/1⅓ tbsp.) lemon juice
⅔ oz. (20 ml/1⅓ tbsp.) cherry brandy
2 oz. (60 ml/4 tbsp.) guava juice
2 oz. (60 ml/4 tbsp.) pineapple juice
few dashes peach schnapps
half a ripe banana
**Blend the ingredients, then add two scoops of crushed ice and blend
again. Pour into a tumbler and serve with a straw.**

Tabu

2 oz. (60 ml/4 tbsp.) rum
1 oz. (30 ml/2 tbsp.) gomme syrup
1 oz. (30 ml/2 tbsp.) cranberry juice
½ oz. (15 ml/1 tbsp.) fresh lemon juice
3 oz. (90 ml/6 tbsp.) pineapple juice
Blend the ingredients until smooth, then pour into a large goblet and serve.

Tail Spin Cocktail

1 oz. (30 ml/2 tbsp.) gin
1 oz. (30 ml/2 tbsp.) sweet vermouth
1 oz. (30 ml/2 tbsp.) green chartreuse
dash Angostura bitters
Shake the ingredients, then strain into a martini glass and serve.

Tapika

3½ oz. (105 ml/7 tbsp.) Chinaco Plata tequila
½ oz. (15 ml/1 tbsp.) Cointreau
½ oz. (15 ml/1 tbsp.) prickly pear cactus syrup
1 oz. (30 ml/2 tbsp.) lime juice
lime slice to garnish
Coat a cocktail glass with Cointreau, moistening the rim, and discard. Sprinkle the rim with salt. Shake the tequila, prickly pear syrup, and lime juice, then strain into the glass. Garnish with the lime and serve.

Tequila Canyon

2 oz. (60 ml/4 tbsp.) tequila
dash triple sec
4 oz. (120 ml/8 tbsp.) cranberry juice
⅓ oz. (10 ml/⅔ tbsp.) pineapple juice
⅓ oz. (10 ml/⅔ tbsp.) fresh orange juice
Pour the first three ingredients into an ice-filled highball glass. Stir, then add the pineapple and orange juices. Stir, then serve with a stirrer.

Tequila Manhattan (see Manhattan, pp. 78–79)

2 oz. (60 ml/4 tbsp.) tequila
1 oz. (30 ml/2 tbsp.) sweet vermouth
dash fresh lime juice
slice of orange to garnish
Shake the ingredients, then strain into an ice-filled old-fashioned glass. Garnish with the slice of orange and serve.

Tequila Mockingbird

2 oz. (60 ml/4 tbsp.) tequila
1 oz. (30 ml/2 tbsp.) green crème de menthe
1 oz. (30 ml/2 tbsp.) fresh lime juice
Shake the ingredients, then strain into a cocktail glass and serve.

Tequila Mockingbird (alt)

1 oz. (30 ml/2 tbsp.) tequila
⅓ oz. (10 ml/¾ tbsp.) green crème de menthe
dash fresh lime juice
lime wedge to garnish
**Pour the ingredients into an old-fashioned glass with crushed ice.
Stir, garnish with the lime, and serve with a straw.**

Tequila Sunrise

2 oz. (60 ml/4 tbsp.) tequila
4 oz. (120 ml/8 tbsp.) fresh orange juice
2 dashes grenadine
orange spiral to garnish
Pour the tequila and orange juice into an ice-filled highball glass. Stir, then slowly add the grenadine. Add the garnish and serve with straws.

Tequila
Sunrise

167

Tequila Sunset

2 oz. (60 ml/4 tbsp.) tequila
1 oz. (30 ml/2 tbsp.) fresh lemon juice
1 tsp. honey
lemon spiral to garnish
Shake the ingredients, then strain into a cocktail glass. Garnish with a spiral of lemon and serve.

Tequini

¾ oz. (22 ml/1½ tbsp.) tequila
¾ oz. (22 ml/1½ tbsp.) vodka
¾ oz. (22 ml/1½ tbsp.) Noilly Prat
dash Angostura bitters
lemon twist to garnish
Shake the ingredients, then strain into a cocktail glass, add the garnish, and serve.

Three Storms Flip
(Ryan Chetiyawardana)

1½ oz (45 ml/3 tbsp.) aged rum
¾ oz (22 ml/1½ tbsp.) Velvet Falernum
⅛ oz (5 ml/1 tsp.) Lagavulin whisky
1 whole egg
pinch salt and pepper
2 dashes Regan's Orange Bitters
nutmeg to garnish
Dry-shake all ingredients without ice. Shake with ice, then double-strain into a cocktail glass. Garnish with grated nutmeg.

Thumbs Up (Mickey McIlroy)

½ oz (15 ml/1 tbsp.) gin
½ oz (15 ml/1 tbsp.) Maraschino
½ oz (15 ml/1 tbsp.) Yellow Chartreuse
½ oz (15 ml/1 tbsp.) lime juice
½ oz (15 ml/1 tbsp.) Aperol
Shake all and strain into a cocktail glass.

Thunder and Lightning

2 oz. (60 ml/4 tbsp.) cognac
1 oz. (30 ml/2 tbsp.) Cointreau
1 egg yolk
4 drops Tabasco sauce
Shake the ingredients, then strain into a cocktail glass and serve.

Tijuana Taxi

1 oz (30 ml/2 tbsp.) gold tequila
½ oz. (15 ml/1 tbsp.) blue curaçao
½ oz. (15 ml/1 tbsp.) tropical fruit schnapps
club soda
**Pour the tequila, curaçao, and schnapps into an ice-filled highball glass.
Fill with soda, stir, and serve.**

Tipperary

1 oz. (60 ml/4 tbsp.) Irish whiskey
¾ oz. (22 ml/1½ tbsp.) dry vermouth
¼ oz. (8 ml/½ tbsp.) green Chartreuse
Shake the ingredients, then strain into a cocktail glass and serve.

Singapore Sling

The writers Somerset Maugham and Joseph Conrad were fans of this legendary, exotic cocktail.

Bartenders are naturally inquisitive people, always playing around with ingredients, seeing just what happens when another ingredient is added to a classic cocktail base. It was therefore inevitable that one of the oldest "simple" cocktails, the Gin Sling, would serve as the base for a range of outlandish experiments.

The Gin Sling itself is Tom highball and takes its name from the German schlingen (to swallow). Slings evolved into the highball family but the name lives on in the Singapore Sling, which was allegedly created in 1915 by Ngiam Tong Boon, the bartender of that enduring symbol of British colonialism, Singapore's Raffles Hotel.

Some gin experts disagree, claiming it dates from earlier. Certainly records show that there was a drink called a Straits Sling in existence before the Raffles recipe, which was a variant on the sling theme with Benedictine, but what we now know as the Singapore Sling appears to have its origins in the Raffles' bar.

Singapore Sling

2 oz. (60 ml/4 tbsp.) Beefeater gin
2 oz. (60 ml/4 tbsp.) fresh lime juice
½ oz. (15 ml/1 tbsp.) Cointreau
½ oz. (15 ml/1 tbsp.) Peter Heering
2 tsp. sugar
dash of Angostura bitters
slice of lemon to garnish
red maraschino cherry to garnish

Pour the gin, lime juice, and bitters over crushed ice in a highball glass. Add the sugar and stir. Then add the Cointreau and Peter Heering, fill up with soda, and serve.

Tokyo Collins (Geoffrey Robinson)

1 oz (30 ml/2 tbsp.) gin
1 oz (30 ml/2 tbsp.) Yuzu sake
1 oz (30 ml/2 tbsp.) grapefruit juice
½ oz (15 ml/1 tbsp.) lemon
½ oz (15 ml/1 tbsp.) sugar syrup
soda
grapefruit slice and cherry to garnish
Build over ice in a highball glass, then stir. Top with soda and garnish with grapefruit slice and cherry.

Tom and Jerry

1 egg
1 oz. (30 ml/2 tbsp.) cognac
1 tsp. superfine (caster) sugar
2 oz. (60 ml/4 tbsp.) dark rum
4 oz. (120 ml/8 tbsp.) hot milk
Separate the egg yolk from the white and thoroughly beat both independently. Stir the beaten egg yolk and white together, then add the sugar and 1 tbsp. of the rum to preserve the mixture. Put 1 tbsp. of the mixture in a heatproof mug, then add the rest of the rum and stir in the hot milk to almost fill the mug. Add the cognac and serve.

Tom Collins

2 oz. (60 ml/4 tbsp.) gin
1 oz. (30 ml/2 tbsp.) fresh lemon juice
1 tsp. superfine (caster) sugar
dash Angostura bitters (optional)
soda
Place the first three ingredients in an ice-filled highball glass, then stir to mix. Fill up with soda. Stir gently and serve.

Tom Fizz

2 oz. (60 ml/4 tbsp.) gin
1 oz. (30 ml/2 tbsp.) lemon juice
1 tsp. superfine (caster) sugar
dash Angostura bitters (optional)
soda
Shake the ingredients, strain into a highball glass, top with soda, serve.

Tom Sour (see Pisco Sour, pp. 146–147)

2 oz. (60 ml/4 tbsp.) gin
¾ oz. (22 ml/1½ tbsp.) fresh lemon juice
½ tsp. superfine (caster) sugar
Shake the ingredients, then strain into a cocktail glass and serve.

Tomahawk

1 oz. (30 ml/2 tbsp.) tequila
1 oz. (30 ml/2 tbsp.) triple sec/Cointreau
2 oz. (60 ml/4 tbsp.) cranberry juice
2 oz. (60 ml/4 tbsp.) pineapple juice
Shake the ingredients, then strain into an ice-filled highball glass and serve.

Top Knotch

1 oz. (30 ml/2 tbsp.) sloe gin
1 oz. (30 ml/2 tbsp.) dry vermouth
½ oz. (15 ml/1 tbsp.) crème de framboise
maraschino cherry to garnish
Pour the ingredients into an old-fashioned glass, then stir. Garnish with the cherry and serve.

Traffic Light

1 oz. (30 ml/2 tbsp.) crème de noix
1 oz. (30 ml/2 tbsp.) Galliano
1 oz. (30 ml/2 tbsp.) Midori
In a shot glass, layer each of the ingredients in turn and serve.

Valencia Royale

1 oz. (30 ml/2 tbsp.) apricot brandy
½ oz. (15 ml/1 tbsp.) fresh orange juice
chilled champagne
Pour the brandy and orange juice into a champagne flute. Fill up with champagne and serve.

Vampire

1 oz. (30 ml/2 tbsp.) gin
1 oz. (30 ml/2 tbsp.) dry vermouth
2 dashes fresh lime juice
Shake the ingredients, then strain into a martini glass and serve.

Vampiro

2 oz. (60 ml/4 tbsp.) tequila
3 oz. (90 ml/6 tbsp.) tomato juice
1 oz. (30 ml/2 tbsp.) fresh orange juice
1 tsp. honey
⅓ oz. (10 ml/⅔ tbsp.) fresh lime juice
half onion slice, finely chopped
few thin slices fresh red chili
few drops Worcestershire sauce
lime wedge to garnish
Shake the ingredients, then strain into an ice-filled highball glass. Garnish with the lime wedge and serve.

Velvet Hammer

2 oz. (60 ml/4 tbsp.) vodka
1 oz. (30 ml/2 tbsp.) white crème de cacao
1 oz. (30 ml/2 tbsp.) heavy (double) cream
Shake the ingredients, then strain into a cocktail glass and serve.

Venus

2 oz. (60 ml/4 tbsp.) gin
1 oz. (30 ml/2 tbsp.) Cointreau
dash gomme syrup
dash Peychaud's bitters
6 raspberries
3 raspberries to garnish

Shake the ingredients, then strain into a cocktail glass. Add three raspberries on a cocktail stick across the glass and serve.

Very Chanilla (Chris Edwardes)

1 oz. (30 ml/2 tbsp.) vanilla vodka
½ oz. (15 ml/1 tbsp.) cherry schnapps
1 oz. (30 ml/2 tbsp.) cherry purée
juice of 1 lime
½ oz. (15 ml/1 tbsp.) gomme syrup
4 griottine cherries

Shake the ingredients, then pour into an old-fashioned glass and serve.

Very Chanilla

Vesper (Vespa)

3 oz. (90 ml/6 tbsp.) Gordon's Gin
1 oz. (30 ml/2 tbsp.) Moskovskaya vodka
½ oz. (15 ml/1 tbsp.) Lillet Blanc
twist of lemon to garnish

Shake the gin, vodka, and Lillet Blanc, then strain into a martini glass, add the lemon twist, and serve.

VIP

1 oz. (30 ml/2 tbsp.) Cointreau
1 oz. (30 ml/2 tbsp.) bourbon
1 oz. (30 ml/2 tbsp.) dry vermouth
slice of orange to garnish

Pour the ingredients into an old-fashioned glass and stir, then garnish with the orange slice and serve.

Virgin Lea (nonalcoholic)

4 oz. (120 ml/8 tbsp.) tomato juice
2 oz. (60 ml/4 tbsp.) passion fruit juice
half yellow pepper, sliced
1 tsp. honey
1 to 2 dashes Worcestershire sauce
**Place the pepper slices in a blender and add juices. Blend on low.
Add the honey, Worcestershire sauce, and ice cubes. Blend on high.
Pour through a strainer into an ice-filled highball glass and serve.**

Virgin Mary (nonalcoholic)

5 oz. (150 ml/10 tbsp.) tomato juice
1 oz. (30 ml/2 tbsp.) fresh lemon juice
1 to 2 dashes Worcestershire sauce
1 to 2 dashes Tabasco sauce
salt
black pepper
1 stick celery
**Pour the tomato juice into an ice-filled highball. Season to taste with
spices. Stir. Add the celery stick as a stirrer and serve.**

Virgin's Answer

1 oz. (30 ml/2 tbsp.) white rum
1 oz. (30 ml/2 tbsp.) brown crème de cacao
1 oz. (30 ml/2 tbsp.) crème de banane
1 oz. (30 ml/2 tbsp.) fresh lemon juice
1 oz. (30 ml/2 tbsp.) fresh orange juice
half of a banana
**Blend the ingredients until smooth, then pour into a large goblet
and serve.**

Viva La Donna!

2 oz. (60 ml/4 tbsp.) tequila
2 oz. (60 ml/4 tbsp.) passion fruit juice
2 oz. (60 ml/4 tbsp.) fresh orange juice
⅔ oz. (20 ml/1⅓ tbsp.) fresh lime juice
Shake the ingredients, then strain into an ice-filled highball glass.

Vodka Martini (see Martini, pp. 104–5)

2 oz. (60 ml/4 tbsp.) chilled vodka
spray of Noilly Prat from an atomizer
olive or twist of lemon to garnish
Spray a chilled martini glass with Noilly Prat.
Add the vodka, the olive or lemon and serve.

Vodkatini (see Martini, pp. 104–105)

3 oz. (90 ml/6 tbsp.) vodka
2 drops dry vermouth
lemon twist to garnish
Pour the vodka into a frozen martini glass.
Splash the vermouth on top of the vodka.
Add the twist of lemon and serve.

Vodka
Martini

Vulga

2 oz. (60 ml/4 tbsp.) vodka
½ oz (15 ml/1 tbsp.) fresh orange juice
½ oz. (15 ml/1 tbsp.) fresh lime juice
2 dashes grenadine
dash orange bitters
Shake the ingredients, then strain into a martini glass and serve.

Wally

1 oz. (30 ml/2 tbsp.) cognac
1 oz. (30 ml/2 tbsp.) Benedictine
2 dashes fresh lemon juice
chilled champagne
Pour the cognac, Benedictine, and lemon juice into a champagne flute. Fill with champagne and serve.

Ward Eight Cocktail

2 oz. (60 ml/4 tbsp) Bourbon
1 oz. (30ml/2 tbsp) Fresh lemon juice
½ oz. (15ml/1 tbsp) Gomme
Dash grenadine
Shake the ingredients, then strain into an ice-filled old-fashioned glass and serve.

Watermelon Smash

1⅔ oz. (50 ml/3⅓ tbsp.) tequila
⅔ oz. (20 ml/1⅓ tbsp.) Limoncello
dash basil syrup
quarter of a slice of watermelon
ginger beer
Shake the ingredients, except the ginger beer, then strain into an ice-filled highball glass. Fill with ginger beer and serve.

Where the Buffalo Roam

2 oz. (60 ml/4 tbsp.) Wyborowa vodka
½ oz. (15 ml/1 tbsp.) Zubrowka bison grass vodka
dash Chambery
ice cubes
blade of bison grass
Coat a shaker with Chambery and discard the excess. Add the ice, both vodkas, and shake, then strain into a cocktail glass. Garnish with the blade of grass and serve.

Whisky Sour (see Pisco Sour, pp. 146–147)

2 oz. (60 ml/4 tbsp.) whisky
1 oz. (30 ml/2 tbsp.) fresh lemon juice
½ oz. (15 ml/1 tbsp.) gomme syrup
Shake the whiskey, lemon juice, and syrup, then pour into an
old-fashioned glass and serve.

Whisky Mac

1 oz. (30 ml/2 tbsp.) Scotch whisky
1 oz. (30 ml/2 tbsp.) Stones Ginger Wine
Pour the scotch and ginger wine into an old-fashioned glass and
serve.

White Baby

2 oz. (60 ml/4 tbsp.) gin
1 oz. (30 ml/2 tbsp.) fresh lime juice
½ oz. (15 ml/1 tbsp.) Cointreau
Shake the ingredients, then strain into a cocktail glass and serve.

White Bull

1 oz. (30 ml/2 tbsp.) tequila
1 oz. (30 ml/2 tbsp.) coffee liqueur
⅔ oz. (20 ml/1⅓ tbsp.) heavy (double) cream
⅔ oz. (20 ml/1⅓ tbsp.) milk
Shake the ingredients, then strain into a cocktail glass and serve.

White Lady

2 oz. (60 ml/4 tbsp.) gin
1 oz. (30 ml/2 tbsp.) Cointreau
1 oz. (30 ml/2 tbsp.) fresh lemon juice
1 tsp. superfine (caster) sugar
1 egg white
Shake the ingredients, then strain into a martini glass and serve.

White Negroni (Wayne Collins)

2 oz (60 ml/4 tbsp.) Plymouth Gin
1 oz (30 ml/2 tbsp.) Lillet Blanc
¾ oz (22 ml/1½ tbsp.) Suze
orange twist to garnish
Stir over ice, then strain into an ice-filled rocks glass.
Garnish with orange twist.

White Russian

1 oz. (30 ml/2 tbsp.) vodka
1 oz. (30 ml/2 tbsp.) Kahlua
1 oz. (30 ml/2 tbsp.) heavy (double) cream
Shake the ingredients, then strain into a martini glass and serve.
Alternatively, layer the ingredients in an ice-filled old-fashioned glass.

Why Not?

1 oz. (30 ml/2 tbsp.) gin
1 oz. (30 ml/2 tbsp.) apricot brandy
½ oz. (15 ml/1 tbsp.) dry vermouth
dash fresh lemon juice
Shake the ingredients, then strain into a martini glass and serve.

Windowlene

1 oz. (30 ml/2 tbsp.) blue curaçao
½ oz. (15 ml/1 tbsp.) white rum
½ oz. (15 ml/1 tbsp.) gin
½ oz. (15 ml/1 tbsp.) vodka
4 oz. (120 ml/8 tbsp.) chilled champagne
spiral of lemon rind to garnish
Pour the ingredients into a highball glass and stir. Add the lemon rind
spiral and serve.

Woo Woo

1 oz. (30 ml/2 tbsp.) vodka
1 oz. (30 ml/2 tbsp.) peach schnapps
3 oz. (90 ml/6 tbsp.) cranberry juice
Shake the ingredients, then pour into an old-fashioned glass and serve.

Woodstock

1 oz. (30 ml/2 tbsp.) gin
1 oz. (30 ml/2 tbsp.) lemon juice
1 tsp. of maple syrup
dash Angostura bitters
Shake the ingredients, then strain into a martini glass and serve.

Woolworth (John Deragon)

2 oz (60 ml/4 tbsp.) Compass Box Asyla whisky
1 oz (30 ml/2 tbsp.) manzanilla sherry
½ oz (15 ml/1 tbsp.) Benedictine
2 dashes orange bitters
lemon twist to garnish
Stir all and strain into a cocktail glass.

Xanthia Cocktail

1 oz. (30 ml/2 tbsp.) cherry brandy
1 oz. (30 ml/2 tbsp.) yellow Chartreuse
1 oz. (30 ml/2 tbsp.) gin
Stir the ingredients in a mixing glass, then strain into a martini glass and serve.

Yellow Bird

2 oz. (60 ml/4 tbsp.) white rum
1 oz. (30 ml/2 tbsp.) Cointreau
1 oz. (30 ml/2 tbsp.) Galliano
2 oz. (60 ml/4 tbsp.) fresh orange juice
Shake the ingredients, then strain into a highball glass and serve.

Yellow Fever

2 oz. (60 ml/4 tbsp.) vodka
⅔ oz. (20 ml/1⅓ tbsp.) Galliano
⅔ oz. (20 ml/1⅓ tbsp.) fresh lime juice
1 oz. (30 ml/2 tbsp.) pineapple juice
**Shake the ingredients, then strain into
a cocktail glass and serve.**

Yellow Monkey

Yellow
Fever

1 oz. (30 ml/2 tbsp.) Galliano
1 oz. (30 ml/2 tbsp.) white crème de cacao
1 oz. (30 ml/2 tbsp.) crème de banane
1 oz. (30 ml/2 tbsp.) white rum
1 oz. (30 ml/2 tbsp.) heavy (double) cream
Shake the ingredients, then strain into a martini glass and serve.

Yellow Rattler

1 oz. (30 ml/2 tbsp.) gin
½ oz. (15 ml/1 tbsp.) sweet vermouth
½ oz. (15 ml/1 tbsp.) dry vermouth
½ oz. (15 ml/1 tbsp.) orange juice
1 cocktail onion
**Shake all ingredients (except cocktail onion) with ice and strain into a
cocktail glass. Add the cocktail onion and serve.**

Yolanda

½ oz. (15 ml/1 tbsp.) brandy
½ oz. (15 ml/1 tbsp.) gin
½ oz. (15 ml/1 tbsp.) anisette
1 oz. (30 ml/2 tbsp.) sweet vermouth
dash grenadine
twist of orange to garnish
**Shake the ingredients together, then strain into a martini glass and
serve with the orange twist.**

Zanzibar

2 oz. (60 ml/4 tbsp.) dry vermouth
½ oz. (15 ml/1 tbsp.) gin
2 dashes fresh lemon juice
2 dashes gomme syrup
twist of lemon to garnish
Shake the ingredients, then strain into a martini glass, add the twist of lemon, and serve.

Za–za

2 oz. (60 ml/4 tbsp.) gin
2 oz. (60 ml/4 tbsp.) Dubonnet
twist of lemon to garnish
Stir the ingredients in a mixing glass, then strain into a martini glass, add the twist of lemon, and serve.

Zombie

¾ oz. (22 ml/1½ tbsp.) gold rum
2 oz. (60 ml/4 tbsp.) dark rum
¾ oz. (22 ml/1½ tbsp.) overproof rum
¾ oz. (22 ml/1½ tbsp.) Cherry Heering
1¼ oz. (38 ml/2½ tbsp.) fresh lime juice
dash grenadine
¾ oz. (22 ml/1½ tbsp.) fresh orange juice
Shake the ingredients, then strain into a highball glass half-filled with ice. Add two straws and serve.

Zombie

Hair of the dog

The easiest way to avoid ever having to refer to this chapter is to not drink too much. However, we've all overindulged at some stage in our lives and suffered the inevitable hangover – the shakes, the headache, the sweats, even a complete loss of memory in some cases. Most hangover symptoms are caused by your body producing too much insulin, resulting in low blood sugar levels. The one part of your body which isn't dried up and screaming for liquid is your brain, which has swollen and is now rubbing against your skull. Apparently, people over the age of 60 don't suffer from as intense a headache as their brains have shrunk, but that's not much consolation if you have 30-odd years to wait. Before a party or even while you're there, there are some things you can do to minimize the effects of one drink too many:

Consuming a glass of milk or a tablespoon of olive oil before you start drinking helps line the stomach and slow down the uptake of alcohol. Drinking plenty of water to slow down the dehydrating effects of alcohol is an even better idea. Alcohol inhibits the release of antidiuretic hormone (ADH) which allows water in the urine to be reabsorbed into the blood. Without ADH we release more water in our urine, thus dehydrating our bodies.

Drink a glass or more of water for every cocktail. If you forget, then drink a pint of water before you go to bed, or if you can't face any more liquid, then at least have one in the morning.

Hangovers come in all shapes and sizes. The type you experience largely depends on what you have been drinking: the more congeners in the spirit, the more vicious the hangover. Be especially cautious of brown spirits like Scotch, bourbon and brandy. Know whether you are sensitive to certain alcohols and compounds within alcohol. Many people get depressed on gin, while others are hopeless after only three pints of beer. Knowing what you can and can't tolerate is another way of preventing a truly bad hangover.

If you forget to carry out any preventative measure before a night of drinking, you can try drinking a cola or eating a fried breakfast in an attempt to raise your blood sugars, but even doctors have to admit that the best way to get rid of a hangover is to turn to a hair of the dog or, literally, "the hair of the dog that bit you."

Here are some personal favourites:

1) The Bloody Mary (see pp. 50–51). There is something about spiced up tomato juice and vodka that just works. The tip is to plan ahead: make jugs of the mix the night before a party.
2) Underberg bitters (those tiny bottles of magic wrapped in brown paper) seemingly blast a hangover out of your ears. What they do in actual fact is get you drunk again, thus numbing the pain of the hangover in the process.
3) If the hangover isn't too bad, you could try a Horse's Neck (see page 99). The ginger ale is great for any residual heartburn and raises the blood sugars, bitters have a tremendous settling effect on the stomach, while bourbon provides the requisite hair of the dog.
4) Pick yourself up with a sour. They freshen the mouth and clear the head. If you want to go gently into the dawn then try a Collins, but remember the best way to fight a hangover is to attack it not to try and persuade it to leave.
5) Try a Campari and orange. The Campari provides the medicinal benefits of bitters, while the orange juice provides a much needed shot of Vitamin C; the whole ensemble tastes wonderful.

Cocktails by spirit

The following pages contain a list of all 500 cocktails featured here, itemized by base spirit or category. Many of the cocktails contain more than one spirit, or fit in more than one category, so they appear more than once.

COCKTAILS BY SPIRIT

Vodka

Including flavoured vodkas

Brandy/ Cognac

All types including Calvados

Rum

All types, including Cachaca

Tequila

All types

ACKNOWLEDGEMENTS

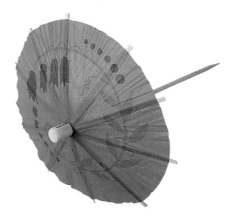

Special thanks to mixologist extraordinaire **Ryan Chetiyawardana**, A.K.A. Mr Lyan, who supplied the cocktail recipes highlighted in the pink boxes, and to **Rebekkah Dooley** of the Callooh Callay Bar in Shoreditch.

The publishers also would like to thank the following people and companies for their assistance in the compilation of this book: **Ivan Jones**, **James Duncan**, and **Karl Adamson**, photographers; **Corinna Thompson** and **Natashia Bartlett,** Oddbins Ltd; **Chris Edwardes** and **Miles Cunliffe**, Blanch House Hotel; **Caroline Fraser Ker**, copy editor.

The publishers would like to thank the following sources for their kind permission to reproduce pictures in this book.

Anthony Blake Photo Library: 16-17; **Gerrit Buntrock**: 51, 65, 79, 93, 105, 119, 133, 147, 161, 171; **Getty Images**: /DiMaggio/Kalish: 8-9; /Photo Disc: 15; **REX/Shutterstock**: /Stewart Cook: 22

Every effort has been made to acknowledge correctly and contact the source/copyright holder of each picture, and Carlton Books Limited apologises for any unintentional errors or omissions, which will be corrected in future editions of this book.